UNLEASHED:
THE GPS TO
HER POWER

NAVIGATE HEALING, PURPOSE, & IDENTITY BEYOND THE STORM

Yvonne Lorraine

Foreword by Dr. Tracy Timberlake

Beyond The Book Media, LLC
Alpharetta. GA
www.beyondthebookmedia.com

The publisher is not responsible for websites that
are not owned by the publisher.

Scripture References:
Unless otherwise noted, all Scripture quotations are taken from the Holy Bible, New International Version® (NIV®).
Copyright © 1973, 1978, 1984, 2011 by Biblica, Inc.™
Used by permission. All rights reserved worldwide.

ISBN: 978-1-966430-08-7 (Print)

Your Guide for the Journey!

Before we begin, I want you to be fully equipped for transformation. This is not just a book; it is a journey. A sacred, powerful walk toward healing, clarity, and purpose. Here is what you'll need to get the most out of it:

- The GPS Journal or Notebook
- To write down reflections, personal revelations, and answers to the prompts provided.
- Highlighter or Colored Pens
- For marking key insights, quotes, and scriptures that speak directly to your spirit.
- Quiet, Sacred Space
- A place where you can read, reflect, and pray without distractions—even if it's just for 10–15 minutes a day.
- Scripture or Faith-Based Companion (Bible or App)
- For cross-referencing biblical principles and adding your own spiritual notes.
- Commitment to a Growth Mindset
- This book will challenge you, but transformation only happens when you're willing to be honest, open, and ready to grow.
- Join this Community
- Share this journey with others or someone you trust for encouragement, accountability, reflection, or shared prayer.
- Bookmark or Sticky Notes
- So you can easily return to your favorite pages, prayers, or strategies.
- A Candle, Oil, or Symbolic Object (Optional)
- To represent your commitment to healing and walking in your purpose. This may serve as a sacred reminder during moments of deep reflection.

Abbreviations & Definitions

As you journey through this transformational guide, you will encounter terms and principles designed to elevate your faith, leadership, and legacy. This section offers a refined glossary to clarify spiritual language, empower deeper reflection, and ensure a seamless reading experience. Consider it your personal reference, crafted to keep you aligned with God's truth while moving boldly in purpose and power.

Abbreviations

- GPS – God's Positioning System — A spiritual compass guiding women back to their God-given identity, purpose, and power.

- NIV – New International Version — A modern English Bible translation commonly used in this book.

Navigation Key Words

- Condemnation - The voice of guilt, shame, or accusation that God has already silenced through Christ.

- Forgiveness - A divine decision to release others and yourself from offense, not to excuse the behavior but to reclaim peace.

- Freedom - Living without the weight of fear, shame, or people-pleasing; moving forward boldly in truth.

- Grace - The unearned favor and divine enablement from God that carries you when your strength runs out and restores what life tried to strip away.

- Healing - The sacred process of letting God mend what life, people, or past experiences tried to break.

- Inner Critic - The internal voice of fear, doubt, or shame that often reflects past pain instead of God's promises.

- Navigate Healing - The intentional journey through inner restoration—spiritually, emotionally, and mentally—guided by grace, where you confront what broke you without allowing it to define you.

- Rest - A sacred act of trust, choosing stillness over striving, surrender over stress, where you let God renew your body, mind, and soul.

- Storm - The seasons of chaos, loss, betrayal, or burnout that threatened to silence you, but instead refined you. The storm didn't destroy you; it revealed your power.

- Stronghold - A mental or emotional grip (often rooted in lies or past trauma) that contradicts God's truth.

- Surrender - Letting go of control and entrusting your pain, plans, and future to God's will.

- Wholeness - Living from a place of emotional, spiritual, and mental integration, not perfection, but healing.

Identity & Empowerment

- Alignment - When your actions, thoughts, and emotions are in sync with your divine assignment.

- Authenticity - Showing up as your true self, healed, whole, and aligned with who God created you to be.

- Boundaries - Healthy, Spirit-led lines that protect your peace, purpose, and personal energy.

- Calling - God's specific invitation to you to rise, lead, serve, or shift for Kingdom impact.

- Identity - Your sacred knowing of who you are in God, not shaped by performance, opinions, or past pain, but anchored in truth, worth, and spiritual authority.

- Legacy - The spiritual, emotional, and leadership imprint you leave on your family, community, and the world.

- Purpose - Your unique calling to impact lives and glorify God through who you are and what you do.

- Unleashed - The divine release of every limitation, label, and lie that once held you back, activating the woman you were destined to be. You no longer perform to prove, but lead with presence, peace, and purpose.

- Voice - Your God-given expression of truth, wisdom, and vision, no longer silenced by fear or shaped by people-pleasing.

- Vulnerability - The courage to be seen, speak your truth, and trust God with your story.

- Your Power - Your God-given authority, voice, and vision, rooted in wholeness, not hustle. It's the strength that rises when your identity is no longer defined by titles or to-do lists, but by truth.

Growth & Leadership

- Clarity - Spirit-led understanding of your next step, your worth, and your role in the bigger picture.

- Courage - Choosing faith over fear, even when you don't feel "ready" or "enough."

- Faith-Fueled Action - Taking intentional steps in purpose, not because you are fearless, but because you are faithful.

- Obedience - Responding to God's direction even when it feels uncomfortable or unfamiliar.

- Rebuild - The intentional act of rising from what broke you—stronger, wiser, and more aligned with who God created you to be.

- Resilience - The God-given strength to rise again after storms, setbacks, or silent struggles.

- Transformation - A lasting shift in your heart, habits, and mindset that reflects healing and growth.

- Vision - A Spirit-led glimpse of what is possible when you walk in purpose and pursue destiny with clarity, confidence, and conviction.

FOREWORD

For a little over six years, I've had the honor of coaching Yvonne Lorraine. Watching her sojourn to her own purpose has been such an honor. Watching her mind shift into fully believing in her God-given greatness… as a coach, this gives me the greatest joy. I've witnessed her courage, her commitment to growth and healing, and her desire to align with God's voice as a leader, educator, and woman. This book is the fruit of that journey. It is raw, real, and rooted in both personal experience and a truth that she was always meant to tell.

Unleashed: The GPS to Her Power is not just another devotional or self-help resource. It is a call to women who are carrying quiet pain behind confident faces. It speaks to the achiever, the leader, the nurturer who has learned to silence her own needs for the sake of everyone else. It speaks to the woman who is tired of looking whole while feeling broken.

Yvonne Lorraine didn't write this because she felt like she had it all together. She isn't writing from a self-concept of perfection. It's from a process. A process that took her YEARS to undergo. You will see that her words are full of honesty and humility. No sugarcoating the struggle here! But you will also notice that she doesn't stop at the struggle either. She offers a clear and Spirit-led path to purpose and power.

I don't believe in coincidences. Having said that, there is a reason this book is in your hands right now. It carries encouragement. It carries answers. It carries truth. And if you let it, it will also carry you into a deeper understanding of who you are, who God is, and what is still possible when you stop surviving and start surrendering.

Yvonne Lorraine's story proves that the storms we are silent in are often the very places God wants to speak the loudest.

Let Him do that.

Dr. Tracy Timberlake

OPENING STORY

There was a time when I didn't have the luxury of falling apart. Life demanded my presence everywhere, for everyone. Not because I wore titles with pride but because I had responsibilities that could not be dropped. I was not trying to be Superwoman. I was simply doing what had to be done, showing up for family, work, ministry, and the call I felt deep in my soul.

But while I stayed strong on the outside, inside, there were times I was exhausted. I did not realize how much I had sacrificed pieces of myself, my voice, and even my health, just to stay available. I kept pushing through, thinking that was what strength looked like. But Romans 12:1–2 began whispering a new truth to me: "Present your body as a living sacrifice… be transformed by the renewing of your mind." That scripture showed me it was not about performance; it was about surrender.

This book was birthed from that place. I want to speak to every woman who has been silently carrying the weight of expectations, duty, and unspoken pain. You do not have to keep it all together. There is freedom in releasing what was never yours to carry and wholeness waiting when you finally say, "Yes"—yes to God's healing, yes to your own voice, and yes to the new you that's rising from within!

UNLEASHED: THE GPS TO HER POWER

Navigate Healing, Purpose, & Identity Beyond the Storm

Chapter Titles and Subtitles:

CHAPTER ONE

Breaking Free: Overcoming Emotional Suppression and Inner Wounds

Healing the Little Girl Within and Stepping Into Wholeness

Let's begin this journey where much of our pain and struggle originates: in the wounds we carry from the past. For many of us, the little girl within is still longing for validation, love, or safety that she never fully received. These unresolved wounds do not disappear with time; instead, they often grow into patterns of emotional suppression that spill into our relationships, leadership, and daily lives. But let me remind you: God did not create you to live in silent storms. He desires wholeness for you, a freedom that comes from healing those inner wounds and stepping into the fullness of who He has called you to be.

Emotional suppression may feel like a form of survival, but it is not truly living. When we bury our feelings, we also bury the joy, connection, and peace God wants for us. God sees the wounds you have carried, even the ones you have tried to hide from yourself. He is not here to judge you for them; He is here to heal them.

Healing begins with honesty. You cannot heal what you refuse to face. That is why it's time to give yourself permission to feel again, to acknowledge the hurt and bring it into the light of God's presence. This is not about dwelling in the pain but about opening the door for God to work in those places you have kept locked away. Jesus said in Matthew 11:28, *"Come to me, all you who are weary and burdened, and I will give you rest."* That includes the weariness of carrying unspoken pain.

As you begin to heal, forgiveness becomes a crucial part of the journey, not just forgiveness for others but also for yourself. Letting go of the past is not about excusing what happened; it's about releasing its grip on your heart. Ephesians 4:31-32 reminds us, *"Get rid of all bitterness, rage and anger... Be kind and compassionate to one another, forgiving each other, just as in Christ God forgave you."* Forgiveness frees you from the chains of resentment and opens the door for God's peace to flood your soul.

Stepping into wholeness does not mean the scars will disappear, but it does mean they no longer define you. Wholeness is about allowing God to take what was broken and transform it into something beautiful, a testimony of His faithfulness and love. That is what God wants for you: beauty, joy, and praise instead of the pain you have carried for too long.

Practical Step:

Take a moment to reflect on the little girl within, the one who has experienced hurt, rejection, or trauma. Write a letter to her, acknowledging her pain and reminding her of the love and healing available through Christ. Then, bring that letter to God in prayer, asking Him to begin or continue the healing process.

This chapter is not just about acknowledging the past; it is also about embracing the future. It is about breaking free from its grip. It's about rediscovering the joy and peace that come from living in the fullness of God's love. As you take this first step, know that you are not walking alone. The One who formed you, who knows every tear you have cried, is walking with you, ready to lead you into healing and wholeness. This is your moment to break free and step boldly into the life He has for you.

Acknowledging and Confronting Emotional Suppression

Healing begins with acknowledging what is hidden. Emotional suppression might feel like a shield, but it's actually a chain, a weight that keeps you from living freely in the joy and peace God intends for you. The feelings you have pushed down, the tears you have refused to shed, and the wounds you have tried to forget don't just disappear. They settle in your heart, shaping how you see yourself and the world around you. But let me remind you: God did not create you to live burdened by the weight of unspoken pain. He is calling you to bring it into His light, where healing begins.

Acknowledging emotional suppression is not a sign of weakness; it is a sign of strength. It is an act of courage. Psalm 34:18 assures us, *"The Lord is close to the brokenhearted and saves those who are crushed in spirit."* God sees the places in your heart where you have buried pain, and He is ready to meet you there with love and restoration.

One reason we suppress emotions is fear—fear of facing the pain, fear of judgment, or fear that we will never recover. But can I remind you? Fear is not from God. 2 Timothy 1:7 says, *"For the Spirit God gave us does not make us timid, but gives us power, love, and self-discipline."* You do not have to be afraid to feel or confront what's been hidden. God has given you the strength to face it, and His love will carry you through.

Practical Step:

Take a moment to reflect on areas of your life where you have suppressed emotions. Write them down, naming the feelings you have buried and the situations that caused them. Then, bring them to God in prayer. Speak to them aloud if you can and ask God to begin the process of healing.

_____

_____

_____

Acknowledging your emotions is the first step to breaking free. When you name what has been hidden, you take away its power to control you. You create space for God's peace to enter and His truth to replace the lies of fear and shame. This is the beginning of your journey to wholeness.

Identifying the Roots of Emotional Suppression

Friend, when addressing emotional suppression, it is important to identify its roots. Emotional suppression does not happen overnight. It is often the result of patterns learned in childhood, past experiences, or messages you have absorbed about what is acceptable to feel or express. These roots can run deep, shaping how you respond to pain and navigate relationships. But identifying them is the first step toward healing.

Some of us were taught that showing emotions is a sign of weakness. Maybe you heard phrases like "Stop crying" or "Be strong." Over time, these messages can lead to a habit of bottling up feelings instead of processing them. Others may have faced situations where expressing emotions felt unsafe or led to rejection, making suppression feel like the only option.

Psalm 139:23-24 says, _"Search me, God, and know my heart; test me and know my anxious thoughts. See if there is any offensive way in me, and lead me in the way everlasting."_ God is ready to help you uncover the roots of your emotional suppression, not to condemn you but to lead you toward freedom.

14

Practical Step:

Take time to reflect on your past experiences. Ask yourself:

1. What messages about emotions did I receive growing up?

_____

_____

_____

2. What situations taught me to suppress my feelings?

_____

_____

_____

3. How have these patterns affected my relationships and well-being today?

_____

_____

_____

After writing down your reflections, take them to God in prayer. Ask Him to reveal any hidden roots of suppression and to guide you in releasing them.

Identifying the roots of your emotional suppression is not about blaming yourself or others. It is about understanding where the patterns began so you can break free. With God's help, you can uncover the truth and begin the healing process.

Recognizing the Impact of Emotional Suppression

Once you have identified the roots, the next step is recognizing how emotional suppression has impacted your life. Suppressing emotions might seem like a way to protect yourself, but it often leads to unintended consequences, strained relationships, physical stress, and a lack of peace. You cannot live fully when parts of your heart are hidden.

Looking back as an adult, I now recognize that I began suppressing my emotions toward my family at a very young age. I found more comfort and emotional safety in my friendships than I did at home. The love I experienced from friends felt more present, more freely given, compared to what I received from family. While I knew my family loved me, expressing that love openly wasn't always easy for them. So, over time, I learned to replace my unmet longing for family affection with the acceptance I found in friendships.

It was not until I became a grown woman with children and grandchildren that I fully understood how the absence of emotional connection in my childhood shaped me. I had unknowingly built emotional walls, equipping myself with internal switches that could turn my feelings on and off with little effort, especially in relationships with men. It was my way of protecting myself from pain.

Long before my deeper walk with God began, one of the first seeds of healing was planted through the words of my grandmother, Juanita Jackson. She told me, "Always love yourself first, because if you don't, no one else will." That truth became an anchor in my life, rescuing me from the trap of settling in emotionally harmful relationships.

Emotional suppression can create walls between you and the people you care about. When you hold back your feelings, it becomes harder to connect authentically with others. Proverbs 4:23 reminds us, *"Above all else, guard your heart, for everything you do flows from it."* Suppressing emotions does not guard your heart; it numbs it, keeping you from fully experiencing the love and joy God intends for you.

Suppression also affects your physical and mental health. Unprocessed emotions can lead to anxiety, fatigue, and even physical symptoms like headaches or tension. God did not design you to carry this burden alone. Matthew 11:28 says, *"Come to me, all you who are weary and burdened, and I will give you rest."* Rest begins when you release what is weighing you down.

Practical Step:

Take a moment to evaluate the impact of suppression in your life. Ask yourself:

1. How has suppressing emotions affected my relationships?

   _____

   _____

   _____

2. What physical or emotional symptoms have I noticed?

    _____

    _____

    _____

3. What might change if I allowed myself to feel and process my emotions?

    _____

    _____

    _____

Recognizing the impact of suppression is not about dwelling on the negative; it's about acknowledging the reality. It's about shining a light on what has been hidden so you can begin to heal. God is ready to help you release these burdens and step into freedom.

Allowing Yourself to Feel Again

One of the most powerful steps in overcoming emotional suppression is allowing yourself to feel again. Feeling does not mean losing control. It means embracing the emotions God gave you as part of your design. Ecclesiastes 3:1-4 reminds us, "There is a time for everything, and a season for every activity under the heavens... a time to weep and a time to laugh, a time to mourn and a time to dance." Your emotions are valid, and God has created a space for each one of them.

Many of us fear that if we start feeling, the emotions will overwhelm us. But can I remind you that God is your refuge and strength? You do not have to face your feelings alone. He is with you every step of the way.

Practical Step:

Begin with small steps to reconnect with your emotions.

1. *Set aside quiet time to reflect on your day and identify how you are feeling.*

    _____

    _____

    _____

2. *Write down those emotions, even if they feel messy or uncomfortable.*

    _____

    _____

    _____

3. *Bring those emotions to God in prayer, asking Him to help you process and understand them.*

    _____

    _____

    _____

Feeling again is an act of courage and trust. It is a declaration that you are no longer hiding from your heart or your healing. As you begin to embrace your emotions, you will find that they no longer control you. Instead, they become a tool for connection, growth, and deeper intimacy with God and others.

Releasing the Pain and Embracing God's Healing

Once you have acknowledged the pain, the next step is releasing it into God's hands. Holding onto pain might feel like a way to protect yourself, but in reality, it keeps you chained to the very things that hurt you. God did not create you to carry those burdens alone. Rest begins with release.

Releasing pain does not mean pretending it did not happen or dismissing the hurt. It means trusting God to take what you cannot carry and to heal what you cannot fix. Your pain is not too big for God. He is not only willing but also able to bind up your wounds and bring you into freedom.

Sometimes, we resist releasing the pain because it feels like letting go of control or admitting defeat. But releasing it is not about giving up. It is about giving it over. It is about saying, "Lord, I trust You to handle this because I can't do it on my own." And God is ready to meet you with His grace and healing.

Practical Step:

Find a quiet moment to pray and physically release the tension. Write down the pain you are surrendering, whether it is a specific wound, a pattern of emotional suppression, or a lie you have believed about yourself.

_____

_____

_____

Now pray, *"Lord, I release this to You. I trust You to heal my heart and carry what I cannot."*

Releasing pain is not about erasing the past. It is about breaking free from its hold on your present. When you trust God with your wounds, you open the door for His peace, joy, and wholeness to flood your life. This is your moment to let go and let Him lead you into healing and freedom.

Surrendering the Pain to God

Once you have acknowledged your emotions, the next step in your journey to freedom is surrendering the pain to God. Holding onto pain might feel like a way to stay in control or protect yourself, but in reality, it only keeps you bound to the past. God invites you to release what you have been carrying so that He can replace it with His peace and healing.

God knows the heaviness of the burdens you have carried, and He is not asking you to carry them any longer. Surrender is not about giving up. It is about giving it over to the One who can handle it.

Surrendering pain begins with trust. You have to believe that God is both willing and able to take your wounds and transform them. Isaiah 61:3 reminds us of His promise: *"To bestow on them a crown of beauty instead of ashes, the oil of joy instead of mourning, and a garment of praise instead of a spirit of despair."* Friend, your pain is not the end of your story. It is the starting point for His restoration.

Practical Step:

Write a letter to God, pouring out your pain, your questions, and your fears. Do not hold back. He can handle it. Then, pray aloud, surrendering each wound to Him one by one. If you feel ready, symbolize the act of surrender by tearing up or burning the letter, knowing that you have placed it all in His hands.

Surrendering your pain does not mean the healing happens overnight, but it does mean you are no longer carrying it alone. Trust that God will meet you in your surrender and begin the work of restoring your heart.

Replacing Pain with God's Truth

When you surrender pain to God, you create space for Him to fill those broken places with His truth. Pain often whispers lies: "You are not enough," "You will never heal," or "You are defined by what happened to you." But those lies lose their power when you replace them with the truth of who God says you are.

God's truth is clear and unwavering. Psalm 34:18 assures us, *"The Lord is close to the brokenhearted and saves those who are crushed in spirit."* He is not distant in your pain. He is right there with you, ready to remind you of your worth and His faithfulness.

Replacing pain with truth begins by meditating on Scripture. God's Word is alive and active, powerful enough to uproot lies and plant seeds of healing. Hebrews 4:12 reminds us, *"For the word of God is alive and active. Sharper than any double-edged sword."* As you immerse yourself in God's promises, you will find that the lies lose their grip, and His peace takes their place.

Practical Step:

Create a list of Scriptures that speak to God's love, healing, and purpose for your life. Write them on index cards or sticky notes and place them where you will see them daily, such as on your mirror, in your car, or on your desk. Each time a lie surfaces, declare God's truth aloud, reminding yourself of His promises.

Replacing pain with truth is a daily practice that transforms your heart and mind. As His truth takes root in your life, you will find the strength and peace to move forward, no longer defined by the pain of the past but by the freedom of His love.

Walking in the Freedom of Forgiveness

The final step in releasing pain is forgiveness, not for the person who hurt you, but for you. Forgiveness is the key that unlocks the chains of resentment and bitterness, setting you free to walk in the fullness of God's peace and joy.

Forgiveness is not about excusing what happened or pretending it did not hurt; it is about choosing to trust God with justice and healing beyond your control. Romans 12:19 reminds us, *"Do not take revenge, my dear friends, but leave room for God's wrath, for it is written: 'It is mine to avenge; I will repay,' says the Lord."* When you forgive, you are not letting anyone off the hook; you are giving it over to God, who sees and handles all things perfectly.

Forgiveness also reflects the grace that has been given to you. The forgiveness God has extended to you is limitless, and He calls you to extend that same grace, not because it's easy, but because it sets you free.

Practical Step:

Start by praying for the person who hurt you, even if it feels impossible at first. Pray for their well-being and for God to work in their heart. If you are not ready to pray for them directly, begin by asking God to help you develop a desire to forgive. Write down their name, and with each prayer, release the hurt they caused into God's hands.

Forgiveness is not a one-time decision. It is a daily choice to walk in the freedom God has for you. As you forgive, you will find that the weight of bitterness lifts, and His peace fills its place. This is where true healing begins and where you step into the abundant life He has promised.

Breaking Free

As we close this first chapter, I want you to pause and reflect on the courageous steps you have already taken. Acknowledging your emotions, identifying the roots of your pain, and beginning the process of releasing it to God are no small feats. These steps are the foundation of your journey toward healing and wholeness.

You were not created to live in the shadows of emotional suppression or to carry wounds that were never meant to define you. The same God who sees every tear you have cried and knows every burden you have carried is the One who is gently leading you into freedom.

Remember, healing is a process, not a destination. There may be moments when the pain feels overwhelming or when the old patterns of suppression try to creep back in. But take heart, God is with you every step of the way. Philippians 1:6 assures us, *"Being confident of this, that he who began a good work in you will carry it on to completion until the day of Christ Jesus."* The work He has started in you today is a work He will see through to completion.

Practical Step:

Take a few moments to write a prayer of gratitude and surrender to God. Thank Him for the healing He has begun and commit to trusting Him as you continue this journey. Keep this prayer somewhere you can revisit it whenever you need a reminder of His faithfulness.

As you move forward, remember that this is just the beginning. There is so much freedom, joy, and peace waiting for you as you step into the fullness of who God created you to be. This chapter may have opened old wounds, but it has also opened the door for God to bring beauty from ashes, strength from pain, and joy from mourning.

Friend, you are breaking free. The chains of suppression and unspoken pain are falling away, and God is leading you into a life of wholeness and peace. You do not have to walk this road alone; He is with you, and He has promised to finish what He started. This is your time to rise, to heal, and to step boldly into the abundant life He has prepared for you.

CHAPTER TWO

Reclaiming Your Peace:
Releasing the Burden of Perfection

Letting Go of the Relentless Need to Appear Perfect

Let me ask you something: how many of you feel like you have to keep it all together 24/7? You've got to be the perfect leader at work, the perfect mom or wife at home, the perfect role model in ministry or business. If that sounds like you, let me tell you, I have been there. I've worn that mask, trying to keep every plate spinning, terrified that one might crash. And you know what? It is exhausting.

This relentless need to appear perfect is not God's design for you. It's a trap, plain and simple. Somewhere along the way, you picked up the lie that your value is tied to your performance. But listen, I am here to remind you that your worth isn't about how flawlessly you can juggle everything. It's about who you are in Christ. God is not asking you to be perfect; He's asking you to trust Him and let Him carry the load.

Can we just take a moment to acknowledge how exhausting it is to always look like you have it all together? Some of you have been driven by an unrelenting need to appear perfect in your leadership, family, and even your ministry. You walk into rooms with a smile that says, "Everything is fine," while inside, you are juggling more than anyone knows. Sound familiar?

Let me tell you, God did not create you to live like that. He did not call you into leadership or business to run yourself ragged, trying to meet impossible standards. This need to appear perfect is not from Him. It's a burden you have picked up somewhere along the way, and it's time to let it go.

The world tells us to strive, hustle, and work harder so we can earn the approval of others or get ahead. But the Kingdom of God operates differently. It is not about what you can do; it's about what He can do through you. 1 Peter 5:7 reminds us to *"Cast all your anxiety on Him because He cares for you."* God is asking you to take off the mask, to stop trying to prove yourself to everyone around you, and to trust that He sees you, loves you, and has called you for a purpose.

When you cling to this relentless need to appear perfect, you are not just fooling others; you are also fooling yourself. You're really fooling yourself. You are convincing yourself that you cannot afford to show weakness, but here is the truth: God does His best work in our weakness. 2 Corinthians 12:9 says, *"My grace is sufficient for you, for my power is made perfect in weakness."* Your imperfections are the very place where God's strength can shine the brightest.

Letting go of this burden starts with being honest with yourself, with others, and with God. It is okay to say, "I do not have it all figured out." It's okay to ask for help. It is okay to rest. You do not have to carry the weight of perfection any longer because the One who is perfect is carrying you.

I remember that, back in our earlier days with my nonprofit organization, my board members expected me to know everything. The problem with that is that I did not know how to do everything. I was really trying to learn how to hear from God and move in the way I believed He was directing me to. So, when I would say, "I did not know something," you would have thought I had said a curse word. And although I was comfortable with not knowing, having the understanding that I could always take time to find out, others found it very uncomfortable.

God is not looking for perfection; He is looking for surrender. And when you surrender, you will find freedom—freedom to be who He has called you to be, without the pressure of performing for others. That's when you will step into the fullness of His grace and purpose for your life.

Recognizing the Root of Perfectionism

Let's talk about where this perfectionism comes from because it didn't just appear out of nowhere. For many of us, the drive to be perfect is rooted in something deeper, such as a need for approval, a fear of failure, or perhaps even a belief that our worth is tied to our performance. Somewhere along the way, you picked up the idea that if you could just do everything right, you would be enough, and everyone would be pleased.

Maybe it started in childhood when praise only came when you achieved something. Or perhaps it is the result of being in environments where mistakes were not tolerated, where excellence was not encouraged but demanded. Whatever the source, it is essential to acknowledge that this mindset did not originate from God.

God's love for you is not based on your accomplishments. Psalm 139:14 reminds us that we are *"fearfully and wonderfully made."* Think about that: God saw you as worthy before you ever did anything. Your value was established the moment He created you, not because of your performance but because of His purpose for your life.

The enemy loves to whisper lies into our minds, telling us that if we just work a little harder, achieve a little more, or prove ourselves to everyone, then we will finally be accepted. But those are just lies. The truth is that God's love for you is unconditional, and nothing you do can make Him love you more or less.

Friend, perfectionism is a trap, and it keeps you running on a hamster wheel of never enough. The more you strive, the emptier you feel. But when you start to recognize the root of this need, when you see it for what it is, that's when you can start to let it go. It is not about ignoring excellence or settling for less; it is about understanding that your identity is not defined by what you do but by who you are in Christ.

So, I want you to take a moment and ask yourself, "Where did this need to be perfect come from? Who or what have I been trying to impress?" Be radically honest with yourself. And then take it to God. Because once you identify the root, He can help you dig it up and replace it with His truth. And His truth says you are already enough!

Breaking Free from the Fear of Failure

Since we are keeping it real, how many of us are afraid of failing? Failure can feel like the ultimate threat to those of us striving for perfection. It is that fear of falling short of letting someone down, of having our weaknesses exposed. But here is the truth: failure is not the end of the world; it's really an opportunity to see the work of God in your life.

When it comes to marriage, my experience has been challenging. People often ask how I have managed to persevere despite life's challenges. For instance, I have been divorced three times, and I am now remarried to my junior high sweetheart. Yes, I remained open to love. Just because my previous husband, who was with me for over 18 years, did not know how to love me does not mean I stopped desiring to be loved.

While I am not proud of having been married several times, I have also learned that staying in a marriage out of fear is unhealthy. Fear of judgment, financial insecurity, or starting over only keeps you trapped in a situation you do not deserve. So, do not let fear hold you in bondage. It is a dangerous path. God's grace allows us to move forward without shame or guilt. God brought me through, and He can do the same for you!

Okay, so let's keep it moving. The fear of failure is often rooted in pride, but not the kind of pride we typically think of. It is not arrogance; it's the kind of pride that says, "What will people think of me if I mess up?" It is this deep-seated concern about others' opinions that keeps us trapped in a cycle of overachieving and overworking.

When you are afraid to fail, you are less likely to take risks, and when you do not take risks, you miss out on the incredible things God wants to do through you. Failure is not the opposite of success; it's often the pathway to success. Think about Peter walking on water. He failed when he started to sink when he took his eyes off Jesus, but Jesus was right there to pull him back up, and He will do the same for you.

Look in the mirror and remind yourself that your worth is not tied to your wins or your losses. It is tied to the One who created you. Failure is not a verdict on who you are; it is an opportunity to grow, to learn, and to lean on God more deeply. Falling is part of the journey, but rising is the promise.

Breaking free from the fear of failure requires a shift in perspective. Instead of seeing failure as something to avoid, start seeing it as a steppingstone. Every failure teaches you something, shapes you, and equips you for what's ahead. God does not waste anything, not even your successes or your challenges.

So, what is holding you back? What dream or step of faith have you been afraid to take because you are scared it might not work out? Let me remind you that God's grace is big enough to cover your missteps. He is not looking for perfection; He's looking for obedience. And when you walk in obedience, even if you stumble, He will be right there to guide you forward.

Embracing Rest as an Act of Trust

Let's talk about rest. Not just physical rest, though that is important, but the kind of rest that comes from truly trusting God with your life. For high achievers, rest can feel like a luxury, something you earn after you have completed everything on your to-do list. But here is the truth: rest is not just a reward; it is a requirement, a command, and an act of worship.

When we refuse to rest, it's often because we are carrying a mindset that says, "If I stop, everything will fall apart." But can I remind you of something? You are not the glue holding the universe together; God is. Psalm 46:10 says, "Be still, and know that I am God." That is not just a suggestion; it's an invitation to release control and let God take His rightful place in your life.

The relentless pursuit of perfection and the fear of failure often rob us of the peace and rest God wants us to have. We push and push, thinking that if we just do a little more, we will finally feel at ease. But that's not how God designed us. He created us to work, yes, but also to rest in Him. The kind of rest I am talking about is that soul-deep rest that frees you from striving.

Here is something else: rest is an act of trust. When you choose to rest, you're saying, "God, I believe you have got this. I do not have to hustle every second of every day because I trust that You are working on my behalf." Isaiah 40:31 says, "But those who hope in the Lord will renew their strength. They will soar on wings like eagles; they will run and not grow weary, they will walk and not be faint." Rest is not a weakness; it's what renews your strength so you can keep going in His power, not your own.

Embracing rest means redefining what success looks like. It is not about how much you accomplish in a day but about how much space you leave for God to work in your life. It means scheduling time not just for tasks but also for stillness, prayer, worship, and simply being in God's presence.

So, ask yourself, where are you running on empty? Where have you been striving instead of surrendering? Start small by taking intentional moments throughout your day to pause, breathe, and remind yourself that God is in control. Rest is not a sign of weakness; it is a declaration of faith. And when you embrace it, you will find the peace and freedom your soul has been longing for.

Redefining Success on God's Terms

Let's be honest. Our culture often defines success in ways that leave us feeling exhausted, striving, and uncertain about ever measuring up. The world says success is about how much you achieve, how flawless you look doing it, and how many accolades you collect along the way. But can I tell you something? That is not God's definition of success.

God's idea of success is not about perfection; it's about purpose. It is about living the life He has called you to live, not the life someone else expects of you. Jeremiah 29:11 reminds us of this: *"For I know the plans I have for you,"* declares the Lord, *"plans to prosper you and not to harm you, plans to give you hope and a future.'"* His plans are not tied to society's expectations but to His divine purpose for your life.

The problem is that many of us get caught in a cycle of striving, chasing goals that may not align with what God has in store for us. We chase career milestones, perfect parenting moments, and the applause of others, thinking these things will bring us peace. But here's the truth: peace is not found in achieving more; it's found in aligning your life with God's will.

Redefining success means letting go of the comparison game. When you are constantly measuring yourself against someone else's highlight reel, you are bound to feel inadequate. Comparison distracts you from your calling and robs you of your joy.

God's version of success also requires surrender. Proverbs 16:3 says, *"Commit to the Lord whatever you do, and He will establish your plans."* Notice the order there—you commit first, and He establishes the plan. Too often, we try to establish our own plans and then ask God to bless them. But true success comes from surrendering your plans to Him and trusting that His ways are higher than yours.

And let's not forget, success in God's eyes always includes rest. Yes, rest is part of the plan. Psalm 127:2 says, *"In vain you rise early and stay up late, toiling for food to eat—for he grants sleep to those he loves."* Overworking yourself to the point of exhaustion is not what God intended for your life. Rest is not laziness; it is a form of obedience.

So, what does this look like in real life? It looks like taking a step back to reevaluate your priorities. Ask yourself, "Am I chasing after God's purpose for me, or am I running after someone else's expectations?" It looks like setting boundaries to protect your time, your energy, and your peace. And it looks like celebrating progress over perfection, knowing that God is far more interested in your faithfulness than in your flawless execution.

When you redefine success on God's terms, you release yourself from the relentless pressure to be perfect. You find freedom in knowing that your worth is not tied to your accomplishments but to your identity as His child. And let me tell you, that kind of freedom changes everything.

Breaking Free from the Comparison Trap

Comparison is the thief of joy. How many times have you scrolled through social media or looked at someone else's life and thought, "Why can't I have that?" Friend, the comparison trap is one of the tenemy's most effective tools to keep us stuck in feelings of inadequacy and discontent. But let me remind you of this truth: God's plan for your life is tailor-made.

God did not create you to be a copy of someone else. Your purpose is unique, your calling is specific, and your journey is yours alone. When you measure yourself against someone else's path, you miss out on the beauty of what God is doing in your own life. Instead of asking, "Why not me?" start asking, "What is God doing in me right now?" That shift in perspective will transform your heart and your outlook.

Breaking free from comparison means fixing your eyes on Jesus and the unique race He has called you to run. Hebrews 12:1-2 says, *"Let us run with perseverance the race marked out for us, fixing our eyes on Jesus."* When your focus is on Him, you do not have time to worry about what everyone else is doing. Your confidence will come from knowing you are exactly where youare supposed to be, doing exactly what He has called you to do.

Letting Go of Unrealistic Expectations

Some of the pressure you feel is not coming from others. It comes from you. How often do we set ourselves up for failure with unrealistic expectations? We want to be the perfect boss, the perfect mom, the perfect wife, all while maintaining the perfect house, perfect body, and perfect reputation. Let me tell you, perfection is a myth and chasing it will leave you exhausted and defeated.

God never called you to be perfect; He called you to be faithful. Notice that it does not say to do everything flawlessly; it says to walk humbly with God. That means showing up, doing your best, and trusting Him with the rest.

Letting go of unrealistic expectations starts with giving yourself grace. This does not mean putting yourself down; it means being honest about what is realistic for you in this season of life. Sometimes, the most spiritual thing you can do is say, "No, I cannot do that right now," and trust that God is okay with that.

Celebrate Progress Over Perfection

Here's the thing about God: He is not keeping score. He is not sitting in heaven with a clipboard, checking to see if you did everything perfectly today. No, God is far more interested in your heart and your progress than in your perfection. Philippians 1:6 says, *"Being confident of this, that he who began a good work in you will carry it on to completion until the day of Christ Jesus."* Did you catch that? God is still working on you, and He is not finished yet.

Celebrating progress over perfection means shifting your focus from what you have not done to what you have already accomplished. Perhaps you didn't complete your entire to-do list today, but did you spend quality time with your kids? Did you take a moment to pray? Did you choose kindness over frustration in a tough situation? Those are wins, my friend, and they matter!

God does not expect instant transformation, and neither should you. Zechariah 4:10 says, *"Do not despise these small beginnings, for the Lord rejoices to see the work begin."* Every small step you take toward living out His purpose is worth celebrating. So, stop beating yourself up over what you have not achieved and start thanking God for the progress you have made. Trust me, you will find so much more joy and peace when you learn to celebrate the journey rather than striving for an unattainable finish line.

Reclaiming Your Peace

As we conclude this chapter, I want you to take a deep breath and reflect on the burden you have started to release. The relentless pursuit of perfection or the striving to meet impossible standards or be everything for everyone was never God's plan for you. He created you to live in His peace, resting in the truth that His grace is sufficient.

Perfectionism whispers lies that keep you stuck: "You are not enough" or "You will only be worthy if you achieve more." But, friend, can I remind you of something powerful? You are already enough because God says so. Your worth is not tied to your performance; it is anchored in His love and grace.

Letting go of perfectionism isn't just about releasing impossible standards; it's also about embracing the imperfections that make us human. It is about reclaiming your peace. When you choose to rest in God's grace, you free yourself to live authentically and joyfully, no longer driven by the fear of failure or judgment. Philippians 4:7 promises, "And the peace of God, which transcends all understanding, will guard your hearts and your minds in Christ Jesus." That peace is yours, friend, as you learn to rest in Him.

Practical Step:

Take time this week to reflect on one area of your life where perfectionism has been stealing your peace. Write down a prayer surrendering that area to God, asking Him to replace striving with trust and anxiety with peace.

_____

_____

_____

As you move forward, remember this: God is not asking for perfection; He is asking for your heart. When you let go of the need to prove yourself and lean into His grace, you create space for His joy, peace, and power to work in your life.

You are enough. Not because of what you do but because of who He is in you. This is your time to release the burden of perfectionism, reclaim your peace, and step boldly into the freedom and grace that God has for you. The journey is not about striving; it is about abiding in Him, and as you do, His peace will guide you into the fullness of life He has prepared for you.

CHAPTER THREE

Fearless and Free:
Conquering Vulnerability

Finding Strength in Your Weakness and Trusting God's Grace

Fear has a way of distorting the truth, making you believe that vulnerability is a sign of weakness or an invitation for pain. It whispers lies that keep you trapped behind walls of self-preservation. But God did not design you to live in isolation or fear; He created you for connection, freedom, and purpose. To truly thrive as a leader and as a woman of God, you must confront the lies fear tells and embrace the truth of vulnerability.

One of the greatest lies fear tells us is that vulnerability equals weakness. This could not be further from the truth. True strength comes from being honest about your struggles while relying on God's grace to carry you through. Vulnerability allows God's strength to shine through your imperfections, inspiring others and drawing them closer to Him. When you stop hiding behind a facade of perfection, you free yourself to live authentically and lead with courage.

Another trap fear sets is the belief that vulnerability will lead to exploitation or rejection. While it is true that not everyone will handle your openness with care, that is not a reason to shut down. Jesus Himself displayed vulnerability—He wept, He shared His anguish, and He opened His heart to those around Him. Yet, He also exercised discernment, choosing carefully when and with whom to share. You can do the same. By seeking God's wisdom and trusting His guidance, you can identify safe spaces and relationships where your honesty will be met with grace and support.

Fear also tells you that vulnerability will diminish your authority, especially as a leader. But remember, leadership is not about projecting perfection. It is about authenticity and service. When you show others that youare human, you invite them to trust you and feel safe to grow under your leadership. Vulnerability is not a weakness; it is a powerful tool for influence and connection.

We are called to live in truth and freedom. Vulnerability aligns with this calling because it fosters humility, builds trust, and strengthens relationships. Jesus exemplified this on the cross, displaying the ultimate act of vulnerability by surrendering everything for us. When you choose to confront your fear of vulnerability, you reflect on His courage and love.

So, how do you begin? Start small. Share a struggle with someone you trust. Pray and ask God to reveal areas where fear is holding you back. Write down the lies you have believed about vulnerability and replace them with God's truth.

_____

_____

_____

Most importantly, remember this: God's grace is sufficient for you. When you step out in faith, He meets you with His strength.

Fear is not your portion, and bondage is not your destiny. Vulnerability is the path to freedom, and freedom is what God desires for you. Step into it boldly, and watch as He transforms your relationships, your leadership, and your life.

A Gateway to Deeper Connection and Healing

When you conquer the fear of vulnerability, you open the door to authentic relationships and profound healing. Vulnerability is not just about sharing your struggles; it is about creating space for God and others to meet you where you are. It is a gateway to the deeper connections and restoration your heart longs for but cannot receive while fear builds walls around it.

Fear tells you that being open will result in rejection or judgment, but the truth is that vulnerability fosters trust and understanding. When you allow yourself to be seen, you invite others into your life in a way that nurtures mutual empathy and support. This is the foundation of meaningful relationships. Consider Jesus. He did not shy away from vulnerability. He shared his sorrows, his joys, and his hopes openly with his disciples, modeling how connection thrives when authenticity is present.

Moreover, vulnerability invites God into the areas of your life you might otherwise try to hide. By being honest about your fears, doubts, and struggles, you acknowledge your need for His grace, allowing Him to work deeply in your heart. Healing begins when you bring what's hidden into the light.

Vulnerability also strengthens leadership. When you are willing to admit your humanity, your challenges, and how you have overcome them, you inspire those who look up to you. They see not just your accomplishments but the faith, resilience, and growth that brought you there. It transforms the way others relate to you, creating bonds built on trust rather than on unrealistic expectations of perfection.

To live fearlessly and free, you must see vulnerability as a strength rather than a liability. It is the key to unlocking the emotional and spiritual healing you need to thrive. By leaning into God's grace and sharing your authentic self with others, you will experience the transformative power of being fully seen and fully loved.

Create Space for Authentic Relationships

It is time to embrace vulnerability and allow others to see the real you, the person God uniquely created, with strengths, imperfections, and everything in between. So often, we get caught up in presenting a polished, "perfect" version of ourselves to the world, hoping to protect our image or avoid judgment. But here is the truth: that carefully constructed image may keep you safe, but it also keeps you isolated. Pretending to have it all together might look impressive from the outside, but it blocks the very connections your heart craves. True relationships are not built on perfection; they are built on trust and authenticity.

When you have the courage to admit your struggles, share your heart, or simply say, "I do not have it all figured out," something powerful happens. You create space for others to do the same. Vulnerability becomes an invitation for a deeper connection, where both parties can grow together. It is a way of saying, "I trust you enough to let you see the real me, and I believe you will do the same." That kind of transparency fosters closeness and mutual respect.

Take a moment to reflect on the people you trust the most in your life. Are they perfect? Probably not. However, chances are they have been honest with you about their challenges, and their willingness to be vulnerable has made you feel safe enough to be real with them, too. That is the beauty of vulnerability; it is the glue that holds strong relationships together.

I remember, while going through ministerial training, being told repeatedly, "You cannot minister to anyone when you have not been through anything because they are not going to want to hear from someone they can't relate to." Well, God took care of that issue with me. I am so relatable and transparent at times that it's very comforting, in a strange way. Like, did you just share that?

Proverbs 27:17 says it best: *"As iron sharpens iron, so one person sharpens another."* This verse reminds us that growth and strength come through relationships, but sharpening can't happen when you're hiding behind a mask. Pretending everything is fine not only hinders your growth but also denies others the opportunity to be part of your journey. When you step into vulnerability, you open the door to meaningful relationships that refine and strengthen you.

Vulnerability is not easy, but it's worth it. It allows you to experience the freedom of being fully known and fully loved, not just by others but also by God. Remember, He created you to live in connection, not isolation. So, take the first step, let the walls down, and watch how your relationships transform when you allow others to see the real, unpolished you.

Unlock Emotional and Spiritual Healing

Hiding your pain does not make it disappear. It only buries it deeper, where it festers and creates more harm. Being vulnerable, especially about your struggles, unlocks the healing that God longs to bring into your life. It is a simple yet powerful truth: healing begins with honesty. When you open your heart, you invite God's presence into your wounds, allowing Him to mend what's broken and restore what feels lost.

I recall Joyce Meyer saying, "You can't heal what you won't admit," and this is so true. Acknowledging your pain does not mean you are weak; it means you are brave enough to confront it and let God handle the parts you can't. Vulnerability is the key that unlocks this process. When you are honest about your fears, doubts, or even failures, you create space for grace to flow. God's healing power is ready and available, but it requires your willingness to bring what is hidden into the light.

Not only does vulnerability allow God to work in your life, but it also helps you process and release the weight you have been carrying. Pain, when left unaddressed, becomes a heavy burden that clouds your joy and peace. However, when you open up to someone you trust, whether it is a friend, a counselor, or even a journal, you begin to feel that burden lift.

Sharing lightens the load because vulnerability helps you face what feels overwhelming, one step at a time.

Vulnerability also reminds you that you are not alone in your struggles. It is easy to believe the lie that you are the only one dealing with a particular issue. But when you open up, you often discover that others have walked a similar road or are willing to walk alongside you. This shared connection fosters a sense of community and encouragement, both of which are essential to emotional and spiritual healing.

Being vulnerable demonstrates your faith in God's ability to work through your pain. It's saying, "Lord, I trust You with my brokenness because I know You are the one who can make me whole." Vulnerability is an act of surrender, a way of letting God take what has been weighing you down so He can transform it into something beautiful. Healing begins when you choose to open your heart to God and others. Do not let fear hold you back from speaking up. Step into vulnerability and experience the freedom of God's restoring power.

Inspire & Lead

Let's be real. Leading with vulnerability takes guts. It is not easy to show people your scars, but can I tell you something? Your courage to be real is exactly what the world needs. When you stop pretending and start leading from a place of authenticity, you give others permission to do the same. You create an atmosphere of freedom where people can be their true selves without fear of judgment.

Here is the thing: leadership is not about having all the answers or being perfect. It's about showing others that you are human, too, and that God's grace is what keeps you going. Jesus did not shy away from vulnerability. He wept, He shared His struggles, and He let people see His heart. And yet, that did not make Him weak. It made Him relatable, approachable, and deeply inspiring.

When you are honest about your journey, the prayers, the struggles, and the moments when you wanted to give up, you show others what it looks like to depend on God. Your cracks do not disqualify you; they are where God's light shines through.

But let me say this, vulnerability is not about spilling everything to everyone. It is about being intentional. Ask God for wisdom about when and where to share your story. Trust Him to guide you to the right people and the right moments because when you share with purpose, your story becomes a tool for healing and hope.

Friend, leading fearless and free means stepping out of the shadows and into the light of God's grace. It is about showing others that God can use anyone, flaws, fears, and all, to do amazing things. So, who in your life needs to see that it is okay to be human? Who needs to know that they do not have to be perfect for God to use them?

When you lead with vulnerability, you do more than inspire; you also foster trust. You set people free. It is not about perfection; it is about pointing people to the One who makes us whole.

Courageously Trusting God with Your Story

So, let's talk about trust. Vulnerability without trust is like trying to build a house on shaky ground, it just does not hold up. To truly conquer vulnerability, you must trust God with your story, including the messy, painful, and unfinished parts. And I know that it is easier said than done. But here is the truth: God already knows your story, and He has been writing redemption into it from the very beginning.

One of the hardest things about vulnerability is the fear that if people see the real you, they will reject you. But can I remind you of something? God loved you at your lowest. Romans 5:8 says, *"But God demonstrates his own love for us in this: While we were still sinners, Christ died for us."* If God can embrace you in your brokenness, you can trust Him to guide you in sharing your story with others.

Trusting God with your story also means believing that He can use it for good. The enemy wants you to think your struggles disqualify you, but God says otherwise. What you have been through —heartbreak, challenges, lessons —are all part of a testimony that can bring hope and healing to someone else.

But let's be clear: trusting God with your story does not mean sharing everything with everyone. It means asking Him to guide you in when, where, and how to open up. Trust Him to lead you to the right people, the ones who will honor your vulnerability and be inspired by your journey.

Here is the beauty of trusting God with your story: it sets you free. When you surrender fear of judgment or rejection, you step into a boldness that only comes from Him. Your willingness to share becomes a testimony of His goodness, a light that shines in the darkness for others to see. And let me tell you, when you let God use your story, it not only transforms others, but it also transforms you.

So, here is my challenge to you: start trusting God with the parts of your story you have been holding back. Pray and ask Him to show you how your experiences, both the good and the hard, can be used to glorify Him and encourage others.

_____

_____

_____

Remember, vulnerability is not about putting your pain on display; it is about letting God turn your story into a message of hope. And when you do, you will see just how powerful it is to lead courageously, trusting Him every step of the way.

Surrendering the Fear of Judgment

Can we get real about one of the biggest barriers to vulnerability: fear of judgment? How many times have you held back from sharing your story because you were afraid of what people might think? Maybe you have thought, *"If they really knew what I have been through, they would never look at me the same."* That fear can feel overwhelming but let me remind you of something powerful: God's opinion of you is the only one that truly matters.

The fear of judgment is a tool the enemy uses to keep you silent, but God calls you to walk in freedom. When you let go of the need to please others and focus on pleasing God, that fear starts to lose its grip.

Here is the truth: not everyone will understand your journey, and that is okay. Your story is not for everyone. It is for the people God has called you to impact. Jesus Himself faced judgment and rejection, yet He remained obedient to His purpose. If He could stand firm in the face of criticism, you can too because the same Spirit that empowered Him is living in you.

41

Surrendering the fear of judgment starts with recognizing your worth in Christ. You are not defined by your past, your mistakes, or even your struggles. 2 Corinthians 5:17 reminds us, *"Therefore, if anyone is in Christ, the new creation has come: The old has gone, the new is here!"* When you embrace that truth, the opinions of others begin to fade into the background.

Practical Step:

Start small. Share a piece of your story with someone you trust, someone who will see you through God's eyes and encourage you to keep going. Each time you share, you will feel the weight of that fear lifting, replaced by the peace that comes from knowing you are walking in obedience.

Remember, your story has power, not because of who you are, but because of who God is. Do not let the fear of judgment keep you silent. When you surrender that fear to Him, you will find the courage to speak boldly, trusting that He is using your story for His glory.

Trusting God to Redeem Your Story

Friend, can I remind you of something today? Nothing in your life is wasted -- not pain, struggles, or even mistakes. When you trust God with your story, you open the door for Him to redeem every piece of it for His glory and your good. The enemy wants you to believe that your past disqualifies you, but God says it is the very thing He can use to display His grace and power.

Think about Joseph in the Bible. He was betrayed by his brothers, sold into slavery, and imprisoned unjustly. Yet, when he looked back, he was able to say in Genesis 50:20, *"You intended to harm me, but God intended it for good to accomplish what is now being done, the saving of many lives."* Joseph's story was not easy, but every trial had a purpose, and so does yours.

Trusting God to redeem your story means releasing control and believing that He can bring beauty from ashes. No matter what you have been through, God is in the business of restoration, and He wants to use your journey to bring hope to others.

But let's be honest, trusting God with your story takes courage. It means letting go of the shame or regret that tries to hold you back. It means choosing to believe that your identity isn't tied to your past but to who God says you are. 1 Peter 2:9 declares, *"But you are a chosen people, a royal priesthood, a holy nation, God's special possession, that you may declare the praises of him who called you out of darkness into his wonderful light."* That is who you are: chosen, cherished, and called to walk in the light of His redemption.

Start by reflecting on the parts of your story you have been hesitant to release to God. Pray and ask Him to show you how He wants to use those experiences to glorify Him and encourage others. Remember, it is not about being perfect. It is about being willing. When you trust God with your story, He will take what feels broken and turn it into something beautiful. And along the way, you will discover a deeper sense of purpose, peace, and freedom.

Sharing Your Story with Purpose

Your story is not just for you; it is for someone else who needs to see what God can do through a surrendered life. When you share your story with purpose, you become a living testimony of God's grace, redemption, and faithfulness. But sharing is not about putting your pain on display; it is about pointing others to the God who has carried you through it.

Let me remind you that every detail of your story has a purpose, even the parts you would rather forget. Your experiences, good, bad, and everything in between, equip you to encourage and support others who are walking a similar path.

Sharing your story with purpose also means being intentional. Not everyone needs to hear every detail, and that's okay. Jesus modeled this beautifully. He shared deeply with His disciples and even more intimately with His closest friends, Peter, James, and John. Trust God to guide you to the right people, the ones who need to hear your story and will receive it with grace.

Your story is powerful, not because it is perfect, but because it's real. When you are willing to be vulnerable, you show others that God's grace is greater than any mistake, fear, or struggle. You give them permission to be honest about their own journeys, and that is where true healing and connection begin.

So, how do you share with purpose? Start by asking God for clarity. Pray for wisdom to know what parts of your story will bring encouragement and hope to others. Then, step out in faith. It might feel uncomfortable at first but remember this: your vulnerability is someone else's lifeline. When you speak about how God has worked in your life, you inspire others to trust Him with their own lives.

Friend, your story is a gift. Do not keep it hidden. When you share with purpose, you glorify God, strengthen others, and remind yourself of just how far He has brought you. And that, my friend, is a powerful legacy to leave.

Embracing Freedom Through Vulnerability

As we have journeyed through conquering vulnerability, I hope you're beginning to see the beauty and strength that comes from letting go of fear and trusting God with your story. Vulnerability is not weakness. It is an act of faith. It's a declaration that God's grace is enough and that your imperfections are a canvas for His glory.

But let's be honest: vulnerability alone is not enough to live a life of freedom and purpose. If we are carrying burdens we were not meant to bear, or if our priorities are out of alignment with God's will, even the most heartfelt surrender will leave us feeling drained and off-balance.

That's where we are headed next, my friend. Burnout and misaligned priorities are two of the biggest obstacles standing between you and the life God has called you to live. They keep you stuck in cycles of overwork, exhaustion, and frustration, making it impossible to fully embrace the joy and peace that comes from walking in His purpose.

So, as we move forward, take a moment to reflect on what might be weighing you down. Are you saying "yes" to things God never asked of you? Are you running on empty because you are trying to do it all? If so, it is time to pause, realign, and let God show you how to live and lead from a place of rest and purpose.

In the next chapter, we will tackle the roots of burnout and discover how to realign your priorities with God's plan. Get ready to release what is holding you back so you can step into the abundant, balanced life He has for you.

CHAPTER FOUR

Burning Bright, Not Out: Realigning Priorities for Balance and Peace

Escaping the Cycle of Burnout and Overcommitment

Let's take a moment to pause and reflect: How often do you find yourself running on empty, overwhelmed by the endless demands of life? Burnout does not happen overnight. It is the result of saying "yes" to - too many things, often without realizing that some of those things were never meant to be your burden in the first place.

Burnout and misaligned priorities go hand in hand. When your schedule is packed with tasks and commitments that do not align with God's purpose for your life, it is only a matter of time before exhaustion sets in. And the pain of that misalignment is not just physical. It's spiritual. It is that nagging sense that, despite all your efforts, you are not doing what you were truly created to do.

But here is the good news: God never intended for you to live this way. If the load you are carrying feels crushing, it is time to ask yourself: Is this the burden God has called me to carry, or am I taking on more than He intended?

Burnout is not just about doing too much; it's also about doing too little. It is about doing the wrong things. It's about prioritizing the urgent over the important, the loudest demands over God's quiet call. It is about saying "yes" out of guilt or obligation rather than out of obedience. And let me tell you, no amount of hustle can make up for being out of alignment with God's plan.

Breaking this cycle requires two key steps: releasing and realigning. First, you must release the things that are draining you and weighing you down. That might mean letting go of commitments that are not aligned with your purpose, learning to say "no" without guilt, and trusting God to fill the gaps. Sometimes, the things that hinder us are not bad in themselves. They are just not part of the race God has marked for us.

Second, you need to realign your priorities with God's will. This means seeking Him first in everything, including your work, your family, and your ministry, and allowing God's voice to guide your decisions. Proverbs 3:6 says, *"In all your ways submit to him, and he will make your paths straight."* When your priorities align with His purpose, you will discover a rhythm of grace that replaces the chaos of over-commitment.

Breaking the cycle of burnout is not about doing less; it's about doing what matters most. It is about living in alignment with God's design for your life, trusting Him to guide your steps, and letting go of the things He never asked you to carry. It's not always easy, but it is worth it. Because when you release the unnecessary and realign with His purpose, you will discover the peace, joy, and balance you have been longing for.

Releasing What No Longer Serves Your Purpose

Let's start with something many of us struggle with: letting go. How often do we hold on to commitments, habits, or relationships simply because we feel obligated? It's easy to think, if I don't do it, who will? But can I tell you something? Carrying burdens you were never meant to carry does not make you faithful; it makes you exhausted.

Releasing what no longer serves your purpose is one of the most freeing things you can do, but it requires trust. You have to trust that God knows what's best for you and that He will provide for the spaces you leave behind. Some things are meant for a season, and when that season ends, it's okay to let go.

So, how do you know what needs to go? Start by asking yourself these questions:

- *Does this bring me closer to God's purpose, or does it distract me?*
- *Am I saying "yes" to this out of guilt or obedience?*
- *Is this draining my energy without producing fruit?*

Jesus Himself modeled this perfectly. He did not try to do everything or meet every demand. Instead, He stayed focused on His purpose, saying in John 6:38, *"For I have come down from heaven not to do my will but to do the will of him who sent me."* If even Jesus, the Son of God, knew when to say "no," how much more do we need to learn this?

Releasing is not about abandoning your responsibilities. It is about being intentional with your energy and time. It's about making space for the things that truly matter, the things that align with God's calling on your life.

48

I know letting go is not easy, but it is necessary. Pray and ask God to reveal what's holding you back. Trust that when you release what no longer serves your purpose, He will fill the empty spaces with His peace, His provision, and His direction. And as you let go, you will find that the weight you have been carrying is not yours to bear and that freedom feels like grace in motion.

Identifying What's Weighing You Down

Before you can release what no longer serves your purpose, you have to identify it. Sometimes, the things weighing us down are not obvious; they are buried beneath routines, expectations, or guilt. But here is the truth: God never called you to carry a load that drains your joy, steals your peace, and keeps you from His best for your life.

Start by reflecting on what feels heavy. Is there a commitment that leaves you feeling resentful instead of fulfilled? A relationship that drains your energy? A habit that keeps you stuck in a cycle of frustration? These are not easy questions, but they are necessary. If something is causing you weariness instead of rest, it is worth taking a closer look.

God often speaks through patterns. Maybe you have noticed that certain activities or commitments consistently leave you feeling overwhelmed or disconnected from Him. Pay attention to those patterns. They are clues that something needs to change. Sometimes, the things that hinder us are not sinful. They are just not part of the path God has for us anymore.

Practical Step:

Make a list. Write down the areas of your life that feel heavy, draining, or misaligned. Then, pray over that list and ask God for clarity. Ask Him to show you what's truly yours to carry and what He is calling you to release.

_____

_____

_____

Remember, identifying what is weighing you down is not about judgment but about freedom. It's about stepping into the life God has for you, free from the burdens that were never meant to be yours. As you uncover those weights, trust that God will guide you in how to lay them down, one step at a time.

Recognizing When It's Time to Let Go

Once you have identified what is weighing you down, the next step is recognizing when it's time to let it go. This is not always easy, especially when the things you are carrying feel important or even necessary. But can I remind you of something? Holding on to everything does not make you stronger. It makes you weary. Strength comes from knowing when to release and trusting God to take care of what you leave behind.

Sometimes, we hold on out of fear, fear of letting someone down, fear of being misunderstood, or fear of losing control. But fear is never from God. Letting go is not about abandoning your responsibilities; it's about trusting that God's power is greater than your own efforts.

Jesus gave us a powerful example of knowing when to say no. Despite the many demands on Him, He often withdrew to pray and rest, aligning Himself with the Father's will. Luke 5:16 says, *"But Jesus often withdrew to lonely places and prayed."* If Jesus, who had the most important mission on earth, took time to let go of the crowds and refocus, how much more do we need to do the same?

Letting go also requires trusting that God has a plan for what you leave behind. When you release a commitment, a habit, or even a relationship that is not serving your purpose, you are not abandoning it. You are placing it in God's hands. Philippians 4:19 reminds us, *"And my God will meet all your needs according to the riches of his glory in Christ Jesus."* Trust Him to fill the gaps and provide for what is truly needed.

Trusting God to Fill the Gaps

Letting go can feel like stepping into the unknown. You might wonder, *if I release this, what will take its place? Will everything fall apart without me holding it all together?"* Let me reassure you: God is faithful in filling the gaps when you trust Him with what you have released.

Sometimes, we hold on too tightly because we believe everything depends on us. But here is the truth: God is the one who holds all things together, not you. Colossians 1:17 reminds us, *"He is before all things, and in him all things hold together."* When you let go of what is weighing you down, you make room for God to work in ways you could not imagine.

50

Trusting God to fill the gaps starts with surrendering control. It means saying, "Lord, I trust You to take care of what I can't." Letting go is not about abandoning responsibilities; it's about releasing them. It's about aligning your life with God's priorities and trusting Him to handle the rest.

Here is another beautiful truth: when you release what is not meant for you, God often replaces it with something better. What you give up for His sake, He transforms into something that brings you peace, joy, and fulfillment.

Practical Step:

Take a moment to pray over the spaces you are afraid to leave empty. Write them down and ask God to show you how He is working, even in the waiting.

_____

_____

_____

Reflect on His faithfulness in the past, how He's provided for you, guided you, and carried you through. Let that build your confidence in His ability to do it again.

Trust may not always be easy, but it is always worth it. God does not ask you to let go so you will be left empty; He asks you to let go so He can fill you with something greater. As you release the burdens He never meant for you to carry, you will discover the freedom, balance, and peace you have been longing for. And in the process, you will see that God's provision is always enough.

Realigning Priorities with God's Purpose

Burnout is not just about doing too much; it's about doing too many of the wrong things. When our priorities are misaligned, even the good things can leave us feeling drained and disconnected from what truly matters. Re-aligning your priorities with God's purpose is the key to living a life that is not only productive but also fulfilling and peaceful.

The first step in realignment is seeking God's guidance. Proverbs 16:3 says, *"Commit to the Lord whatever you do, and he will establish your plans."* Too often, we rush into commitments, projects, or even relationships without pausing to ask, "Lord, is this Your will for me?" Taking the time to seek His direction allows you to focus on what He is calling you to in this season rather than chasing after everything that demands your attention.

Misaligned priorities often happen when we confuse what is urgent with what is important. The world will always pull you toward what feels urgent -- work deadlines, social obligations, or even the pressure to say "yes" to everything. But God calls you to focus on what is truly important -- your relationship with Him, your health, your family, and the specific purpose He's placed on your life. Matthew 6:33 reminds us, *"But seek first his kingdom and his righteousness, and all these things will be given to you as well."* When you prioritize Him, everything else falls into place.

Realignment also means learning to say "no" without guilt. My Friend, your "yes" is powerful, and it should be reserved for what aligns with God's purpose for you. Jesus Himself said "no" to certain demands, choosing instead to focus on His mission. Like Jesus, you can say "no" with confidence when it means staying true to your calling.

Practical Step:

Take inventory of your current commitments. Write them down and ask yourself:

- *Does this align with the purpose God has for me right now?*
- *Is this drawing me closer to Him or pulling me away?*
- *Am I doing this out of obedience or obligation?*

_____

_____

_____

As you begin to realign your priorities, you will notice something beautiful: your energy will return, your peace will grow, and your sense of purpose will become clearer. Realignment is not about doing less but about doing what matters most. And when you do that, you will find the balance and freedom you have been longing for.

Seeking God's Guidance Before You Commit

One of the most common reasons our priorities become misaligned is because we jump into commitments without first seeking God's guidance. It's easy to say "yes" to what seems like a good opportunity or an urgent need, but just because it's good doesn't mean it's God's will for you.

Seeking God's guidance before you commit is an act of faith and trust. When you pause to ask God for direction, you open the door for Him to lead you into what aligns with His purpose for your life.

The challenge is often slowing down long enough to ask. We live in a fast-paced world where decisions are made on the fly, and the pressure to act quickly can feel overwhelming. But taking a moment to pray, reflect, and seek God's wisdom can save you from committing to something that will drain your energy and pull you away from His plan. James 1:5 reminds us, *"If any of you lacks wisdom, you should ask God, who gives generously to all without finding fault, and it will be given to you."*

Practical Step:

Before saying "yes" to any new commitment, ask yourself these three questions:

1. *Have I prayed about this and sought God's will?*
2. *Does this align with the purpose God has called me to in this season?*
3. *Will this bring me closer to Him, or will it create unnecessary stress and distraction?*

Jesus modeled this beautifully. Before making major decisions, like choosing His disciples, He spent time in prayer. Luke 6:12 says, *"One of those days Jesus went out to a mountainside to pray and spent the night praying to God."* If Jesus needed to seek the Father's guidance, how much more do we?

When you commit without consulting God, you risk stepping into something that isn't meant for you. But when you take the time to seek Him first, you will find clarity, peace, and confidence in your decisions. Let His voice guide you and watch how your priorities begin to align with His perfect plan.

Distinguishing the Important from the Urgent

Have you ever felt like you were constantly putting out fires, running from one urgent task to the next, yet still feeling like you are not making progress? That's the trap of prioritizing the urgent over the important. The truth is not everything demanding your attention deserves your time, and learning to distinguish between the two is essential to realigning your priorities with God's purpose.

The world is loud, constantly pulling at you with deadlines, expectations, and opportunities. But God calls you to something deeper. In Luke 10:38-42, we see Martha distracted by the urgent demands of serving while Mary sits at Jesus' feet, choosing what is truly important. Jesus gently reminds Martha, *"You are worried and upset about many things, but few things are needed—or indeed only one."* Friend, the same is true for us. When we focus on what's truly important, spending time with God, investing in meaningful relationships, and walking in our purpose, the noise of urgency fades away.

Distinguishing those important things from the urgent ones begins with intentional reflection. Ask yourself:

1. *Is this task or commitment aligned with God's calling for me in this season?*
2. *Does this bring lasting value, or is it simply a short-term demand?*
3. *Am I choosing this out of fear, guilt, or pressure rather than obedience?*

Learning to prioritize what is important does not mean ignoring urgent needs. It means giving them their proper place. Jesus often responded to urgent needs, like healing the sick or feeding the hungry, but He never let those demands distract Him from His greater mission. He took time to pray, rest, and refocus, ensuring His priorities stayed aligned with the Father's will.

Practical Step:

Create space in your daily schedule for what is truly important. That might mean starting your day with prayer and Scripture, setting aside time for meaningful connections with loved ones, or carving out moments to rest and recharge. As you prioritize, you will find it easier to handle the urgent without feeling overwhelmed.

Remember, when you focus on what matters most, you honor God and create a life of purpose and peace. Do not let the demands of urgency rob you of the joy that comes from living in alignment with His will. Choose what is important and trust Him to help you handle the rest.

Learning to Say "No" with Grace

One of the hardest lessons to learn, but one of the most liberating, is the power of saying "no." Overcommitment is often the result of feeling obligated to say "yes" to everything—every request, every opportunity, every need. But can I remind you of something? Your "yes" is valuable, and it should only be given to what aligns with God's purpose for your life.

Saying "no" is not about being selfish; it's about being wise. Ephesians 5:15-17 says, *"Be very careful, then, how you live—not as unwise but as wise, making the most of every opportunity, because the days are evil. Therefore, do not be foolish, but understand what the Lord's will is."* Living wisely means guarding your time and energy for the things that matter most, even if it means disappointing others.

Sometimes, we say "yes" out of fear of letting people down, fear of missing out, or fear of being misunderstood. But saying "yes" to everything often leads to exhaustion and resentment, robbing you of the joy God intended for your work. Jesus Himself understood the importance of saying "no." In Mark 1:35-38, after spending time in prayer, He chose to leave a crowd of people who wanted Him to stay, saying, *"Let us go somewhere else—to the nearby villages— so I can preach there also. That is why I have come."* Jesus didn't let the demands of others dictate His mission, and neither should you.

Learning to say "no" with grace starts with clarity about your priorities. When you are confident about what God has called you to in this season, it becomes easier to recognize which opportunities align with His plan and which do not.

Practical Step:

Before agreeing to any new commitment, pause and ask yourself:

1. *Does this align with God's purpose for me right now?*
2. *Am I saying "yes" out of guilt, fear, or pressure?*
3. *Will this bring peace and fruitfulness, or will it add unnecessary stress?*

Once you decide to say "no," do it with kindness and confidence. You do not have to over-explain or feel guilty. A simple, gracious response like, "Thank you for thinking of me, but I will not be able to commit to this right now," is enough. Trust that God will honor your boundaries and provide for your needs in another way.

Your time and energy are gifts from God, and how you use them matters. Saying "no" is not closing a door; it's keeping the door open for what He has planned for you. When you learn to say "no" with grace, you protect your peace, honor your priorities, and create space for the fullness of what God has for you.

Restoring the Rhythm

As we have journeyed through the cycles of burnout and misaligned priorities, I hope you have felt a glimmer of hope stirring within you. Please know that burnout is not your destiny, and living a life of overcommitment is not the plan God has for you. He is calling you to something better, a rhythm of grace, purpose, and peace.

Letting go of what no longer serves your purpose, realigning your priorities, and learning to say "no" with grace are not just strategies; they are acts of faith. They are declarations that you trust God to guide your steps, to fill the gaps, and to equip you for the things He's called you to do.

Remember, it is not about doing less; it is about doing what matters most. It's about walking in alignment with God's will and experiencing the freedom that comes from releasing the burdens you were never meant to carry. Psalm 37:23 reminds us, *"The Lord makes firm the steps of the one who delights in him."* Friend, as you delight in Him and seek His guidance, He will lead you into a life of balance and fulfillment.

But the journey does not stop here. Burnout often leaves deeper wounds, emotional exhaustion, self-doubt, and even questioning your worth. These scars can affect how you see yourself, your relationships, and your ability to lead with confidence. Take a moment to breathe, reflect, and thank God for the work He has already done in your heart. You are stepping into a new rhythm, a rhythm that will allow you to thrive and not just survive. Let's continue this journey together.

CHAPTER FIVE

**From Empty to Overflow: Escaping
the Trap of Self-Sacrifice**

Silencing the Inner Critic and Serving From a Place of Joy

Let's think about how often you pour yourself out for others, only to feel empty, unappreciated, and unseen. Self-sacrifice is a beautiful expression of love and service when done with the right heart and balance. But too often, we find ourselves trapped in a cycle of giving to everyone else while neglecting our own needs and purpose. And to make it worse, there is often a relentless inner critic whispering lies that keep us stuck in guilt, shame, or feelings of inadequacy.

God did not design you to live this way. The sacrifice He desires is not about depleting yourself until there is nothing left; it's about giving from the overflow of His love and strength. Romans 12:1 says, *"Therefore, I urge you, brothers and sisters, in view of God's mercy, to offer your bodies as a living sacrifice, holy and pleasing to God—this is your true and proper worship."* True self-sacrifice aligns with worship; it brings joy and purpose, not exhaustion and bitterness.

The trap of self-sacrifice without fulfillment begins when we prioritize others at the expense of our relationship with God and ourselves. It's giving from a place of obligation or fear rather than obedience and love. Friend, let me remind you: God never asks you to pour out what He has not first filled. If you are running on empty, it's time to reconnect with the Source.

And then there is the inner critic, that harsh voice that tells you that you are not doing enough, that you will never measure up, or that your efforts are not good enough. That voice does not come from God. His Word says in Romans 8:1, *"Therefore, there is now no condemnation for those who are in Christ Jesus."* The inner critic is the enemy's attempt to rob you of your peace and purpose, but you have the power to silence it by replacing lies with truth.

Escaping this trap requires two key shifts: redefining self-sacrifice and rewriting the narrative of your inner critic. First, redefine self-sacrifice as an act of love and service that honors both God and you. This means setting boundaries, prioritizing self-care, and giving from a place of abundance rather than depletion. Jesus modeled this balance perfectly. He served tirelessly, yet He often withdrew to pray, rest, and reconnect with the Father. Luke 5:16 says, *"But Jesus often withdrew to lonely places and prayed."* If Jesus needed time to recharge, so do you.

Second, rewrite the narrative of your inner critic. When those negative voices arise, counter them with God's truth. If the critic says, "You are not enough," remind yourself of Psalm 139:14: *"I praise you because I am fearfully and wonderfully made."* If it says, "You will never succeed," declare Philippians 4:13: *"I can do all this through him who gives me strength."* Speak life over yourself, friend, because your words have power.

True fulfillment comes not from endless sacrifice but from aligned, intentional living. When you escape the trap of over-sacrifice and silence the inner critic, you create space for joy, peace, and purpose. You start living the life God has called you to, one that honors Him, serves others, and nurtures your soul.

It's time to stop running on empty and start living from overflow. Let's redefine what it means to give, silence the lies that hold you back, and step boldly into the freedom and purpose God has for you.

Redefining Self-Sacrifice as Aligned Service

So, let's talk about self-sacrifice, the kind that feels noble but often leaves you drained, frustrated, and wondering if your efforts even matter. Self-sacrifice in its purest form is a reflection of God's love, but somewhere along the way, many of us lose balance. We give out of obligation or fear rather than obedience and joy, and the result is burnout instead of fulfillment.

One of the biggest traps of misaligned sacrifice is saying "yes" to everything because you feel you should. But friend, can I remind you that saying "no" is not selfish? Jesus, the ultimate example of self-sacrifice, said "no" when it was necessary to stay focused on His mission. Jesus knew when to step away and when to prioritize His purpose, and you can, too.

Redefining self-sacrifice begins with understanding that your service is most impactful when it flows from alignment with God's plan. This requires prayer and discernment.

Another essential part of aligned service is setting boundaries. Take note that boundaries are not barriers. They are bridges that protect your ability to serve effectively. When you overextend yourself, you risk giving less than your best to the people and tasks that matter most. Proverbs 4:23 says, *"Above all else, guard your heart, for everything you do flows from it."*

Guarding your heart means protecting your energy, your time, and your focus so you can give your best where it matters most.

Finally, remember that self-care is part of self-sacrifice. Jesus often withdrew to rest, pray, and recharge. Taking care of yourself is not selfish. It's a way to honor God by stewarding the body and spirit He has given you.

When you redefine self-sacrifice as aligned service, you will find that giving no longer feels like a burden but a blessing. You will serve from a place of joy, knowing that your efforts are aligned with God's purpose, and that alignment will lead to the fulfillment your heart has been longing for.

Serving from Overflow, Not Exhaustion

Think about how many times you have said, "I'll rest later," or "I will take care of myself once everyone else is okay'? It's easy to fall into the mindset that self-sacrifice means giving until you are empty. But can I remind you of something powerful? God never asked you to pour out from emptiness. True, meaningful service comes from the overflow of His love and strength in your life.

Jesus gave us the perfect example. He served tirelessly, healing, teaching, and ministering to countless people. But He also often took time to rest and recharge. Notice that word often. Even Jesus, with His divine mission, knew the importance of filling Himself up before pouring into others.

Serving from overflow begins with your connection to God. John 15:5 says, "I am the vine; you are the branches. If you remain in me and I in you, you will bear much fruit; apart from me you can do nothing." When you prioritize your relationship with God through prayer, worship, and time in His Word, you stay connected to the source of your strength. That connection allows you to serve with joy and peace, even in challenging seasons.

Another aspect of serving from overflow is being intentional about rest. Remember, rest is not laziness; it's obedience. Exodus 20:8-10 reminds us of the Sabbath, a day set aside for rest and worship. When you honor God by resting, you are acknowledging that He is in control, not you. Rest

CHAPTER FIVE: From Empty to Overflow.

allows you to recharge physically, emotionally, and spiritually so you can serve with clarity and purpose.

Practical Step:

Take inventory of your daily rhythms. Are you creating space for God to refill you? Are you setting aside time to rest and recharge? Start small, schedule 15 minutes each day to spend in prayer, or simply be still before God. Over time, let that space grow.

Serving from overflow is not just about what you give to others; it's about how you honor God with your life. When you pour out from a full cup, your service becomes an expression of joy, love, and purpose, not obligation or exhaustion. And that kind of service changes everything.

Setting Boundaries to Protect Your Purpose

Boundaries are not meant to be walls but intentional limits that protect your energy, time, and focus so you can serve with clarity and purpose. Too often, we think that saying "yes" to everything is a sign of faithfulness. However, overcommitting does not make you a better servant; it makes you a burnt-out one. God never asked you to do it all. Instead, He calls you to be intentional about what you say "yes" to and to guard the purpose He has placed in your life.

Setting boundaries starts with understanding your priorities. You cannot protect what you have not defined. Ask yourself:

1. *What has God called me to focus on in this season?*
2. *What commitments or tasks align with His purpose for my life?*
3. *What is draining my energy without producing fruit?*

Once you have identified your priorities, practice saying "no" with grace. Saying "no" does not mean rejecting people. It means honoring the mission God has given you. Proverbs 4:23 says, *"Above all else, guard your heart, for everything you do flows from it."* Guarding your heart includes protecting your time and energy so you can give your best where it matters most.

61

Practical Step:

Start small. Identify one area where you have overcommitted and prayerfully consider how you can step back. When a new request comes your way, pause before answering. Take time to pray, reflect, and ensure it aligns with your purpose. You do not have to give an answer immediately, and it is okay to say, "Let me pray about it."

Boundaries are not barriers. They are bridges that help you serve effectively without losing yourself in the process. When you set healthy boundaries, you create space for God to work through you in powerful, intentional ways. And when your "yes" aligns with His will, your service becomes a joy, not a burden.

Serving with Joy by Staying in Your Lane

Have you ever felt stretched thin, trying to do everything for everyone, only to end up feeling frustrated and unfulfilled? That's what happens when you stray from your lane, the unique purpose God designed just for you. Serving with joy requires staying in alignment with the specific calling and gifts God has placed in your life. When you stay in your lane, you will find freedom, peace, and effectiveness in your service.

God created you with a specific purpose in mind. Your lane is not an afterthought; it is intentional, and when you embrace it, you are walking in alignment with His plan.

The trouble begins when we compare ourselves to others, thinking we need to do what they are doing or measure up to their standards. But can I remind you of something? God did not create you to run someone else's race. Hebrews 12:1 says, *"Let us run with perseverance the race marked out for us."* Your lane is uniquely yours, and when you try to do it all or imitate someone else, you miss out on the joy and fulfillment that comes from staying true to your calling.

Staying in your lane also means honoring the gifts God has given you. Romans 12:6-8 reminds us, *"We have different gifts, according to the grace given to each of us."* Whether your gift is teaching, serving, encouraging, or leading, your role is vital to the body of Christ. Trying to operate outside your gifting not only drains you but also diminishes the impact you were meant to have.

Practical Step:

Take time to reflect on your gifts and calling. Ask yourself:

1. *What comes naturally to me and brings me joy when I serve?*
2. *Where have I seen God use me most effectively in the past?*
3. *Am I stepping into roles that align with my strengths, or am I taking on tasks that leave me feeling overwhelmed and out of place?*

Friend, when you stay in your lane, you honor the God who created you. You serve with joy and confidence, knowing that your work matters and that it's making an eternal impact. Instead of spreading yourself thin, you focus on doing what you were uniquely designed to do, and that is where the magic happens.

Let go of the need to do it all and embrace the freedom of doing what God has called you to do. When you serve from your lane, you will experience the joy, fulfillment, and fruitfulness that only comes from being in alignment with His perfect plan.

Silencing the Inner Critic with God's Truth

What about that voice in your head, the one that whispers, *"You are not enough," "You are failing,"* or *"You will never measure up."* That voice, the inner critic, can feel overwhelming and relentless. But here is the truth: those words do not come from God. They are lies designed to keep you stuck in fear, self-doubt, and shame. God's voice is one of love, encouragement, and truth, and learning to silence the inner critic is essential to walking in the freedom He has for you.

The inner critic often thrives on perfectionism and fear. It magnifies your mistakes, compares you to others, and convinces you that your value is tied to your performance. But God's Word tells a different story. If you are in Christ, there is no condemnation, none. Your worth is not based on what you do but on who you are as God's beloved daughter.

Silencing the inner critic starts with recognizing its lies and replacing them with God's truth. For every negative thought, there is a promise in Scripture that speaks life and hope. When the critic says, "You are not enough," respond with Psalm 139:14: *"I praise you because I am*

63

fearfully and wonderfully made." When it says, "You are a failure," declare Philippians 4:13: "*I can do all this through him who gives me strength.*" Speaking God's truth over your life is a powerful weapon against the lies.

It is also important to identify the root of the inner critic. Often, it stems from past hurts, unrealistic expectations, or words spoken over you that do not align with God's plan. Friend, you do not have to carry those wounds any longer. Isaiah 61:1 reminds us, "*He has sent me to bind up the brokenhearted, to proclaim freedom for the captives and release from darkness for the prisoners.*" God wants to heal those areas of your heart and free you from the critical voice that holds you captive.

Practical Step:

Start a truth journal. Each time the inner critic speaks, write down the lie and counter it with Scripture. Keep those truths close and revisit them often. Over time, you will find that God's voice becomes louder than the critics.

Silencing the inner critic is not about pretending it does not exist; it's about choosing to believe God's truth over its lies. When you align your thoughts with His Word, you will discover confidence and peace that cannot be shaken. You will step boldly into your calling, free from the chains of self-doubt and fear, and fully embrace the life He has for you.

Recognizing the Lies of the Inner Critic

Before you can silence the inner critic, you must first recognize its voice. The inner critic thrives on subtle lies, disguising them as truths that seem logical or even justified. But let me remind you of something: God's voice never condemns or tears you down. If the voice in your mind is filled with guilt, shame, or unworthiness, it is not from God.

The inner critic often disguises itself as perfectionism or fear. It might sound like, "If you don't do everything perfectly, you are a failure," or "You are not good enough for this calling." These are lies designed to paralyze you and keep you from walking in God's purpose. John 10:10 reminds us, "The thief comes only to steal and kill and destroy; I have come that they may have life, and have it to the full." Friend, the inner critic is the thief, and its lies are meant to steal your joy and destroy your confidence.

Practical Step:

Start listening closely to your thoughts. When a negative or self-critical thought arises, pause and ask:

1. *Does this align with God's Word?*
2. *Is this thought building me up or tearing me down?*
3. *Would I say this to someone I love?*

Recognizing the lies is the first step to silencing them. Once you identify them, you can begin to replace them with God's truth. Remember, the inner critic may speak loudly, but it does not speak the truth. God's Word is your ultimate authority, and His voice always leads to freedom and peace.

Replacing Lies with God's Truth

Once you have identified the lies of the inner critic, the next step is to counter them with God's truth. Scripture is your most powerful weapon in this battle. Ephesians 6:17 calls the Word of God *"the sword of the Spirit."* When you speak His truth over your life, you cut through the lies and declare victory over the voice that seeks to tear you down.

For every lie the inner critic whispers, there is a promise in God's Word to replace it. If it says, "You're not enough," respond with 2 Corinthians 12:9: *"My grace is sufficient for you, for my power is made perfect in weakness."* If it says, "You'll never succeed," counter it with Philippians 4:13: *"I can do all this through him who gives me strength."* The key is to arm yourself with Scripture so that when the lies arise, you are ready to fight back.

Practical Step:

Create a list of Scriptures that speak directly to the areas where you struggle most. Write them down, memorize them, and keep them close -- on your phone, your desk, or your bathroom mirror. The more you fill your mind with God's truth, the quieter the inner critic will become.

Replacing lies with truth is a daily practice. It's about retraining your mind to align with God's perspective instead of the enemy's lies. As you do this, you will find a renewed sense of confidence and peace, knowing that your identity is firmly rooted in Him.

Breaking Free from the Power of Past Wounds

The inner critic often gains its strength from unresolved wounds, words spoken over you, past failures, or experiences that left a mark on your heart. But friend, can I remind you? You do not have to carry the weight of those wounds any longer. God's desire is to heal your heart and free you from the lies that have taken root.

Practical Step:

Take time in prayer to identify the wounds feeding your inner critic. Write them down and ask God to reveal His truth about each one. For example, if someone told you, "You will never be good enough," ask God to show you His perspective. His Word says in Psalm 139:14, "*I praise you because I am fearfully and wonderfully made.*"

Friend, breaking free from past wounds takes courage, but it is worth it. As you allow God to heal those places, you will find the inner critic losing its grip on your mind and heart. And in its place, you will hear His voice—gentle, loving, and full of truth, guiding you into the freedom and confidence you were always meant to walk in.

From Self-Doubt to God-Confidence

As we have explored the traps of self-sacrifice without fulfillment and the relentless voice of the inner critic, I hope you have begun to see that you were never meant to live in these cycles of exhaustion and self-doubt. God did not call you to a life of depletion or to a battle against a voice that constantly questions your worth. Instead, He calls you to a life of purpose, balance, and confidence rooted in His truth.

Escaping these traps starts with redefining self-sacrifice, not as losing yourself but as aligning your service with God's purpose. It's about setting boundaries that protect your energy and staying in your lane, where you can serve with joy and fulfillment. When you embrace this, you give from a place of overflow, reflecting on His love and strength in everything you do.

Silencing the inner critic is the next step to freedom. The lies that say, "You are not enough" or "You will never measure up" are nothing but distractions from the truth of who God says you are. When you replace those lies with His Word and allow Him to heal the wounds that feed them, you step into a confidence that nothing can shake, a God-confidence that empowers you to live boldly and unapologetically as the woman He created you to be.

But, friend, this is not a one-time decision. It is a daily journey of trust and surrender. Each time you feel the pull to overcommit or the sting of self-doubt, pause. Reflect. Ask God to realign your heart with His truth. And remember, you are not alone in this journey. Psalm 46:1 reminds us, *"God is our refuge and strength, an ever-present help in trouble."* He is with you, guiding you, strengthening you, and cheering you on.

As we move into the next chapter, we will dive deeper into the power of authentic leadership, how to lead with purpose, vulnerability, and grace, and how to inspire others by walking boldly in your calling. Get ready to step into the fullness of what God has for you, friend. This is only the beginning of your transformation.

CHAPTER SIX

Chains to Freedom: Releasing Past Hurts and Embracing Forgiveness

Letting Go of Toxic Relationships and Trusting God for Healing

I know letting go of past hurts is one of the hardest but most freeing things you can do. It is not just about releasing the person who hurt you; it is also about releasing yourself from the pain that has been weighing you down. Forgiveness does not excuse the offense; it empowers you to live freely and no longer be tethered to bitterness or resentment.

God sees the depths of your pain, and He does not minimize it. Psalm 56:8 reminds us, *"You keep track of all my sorrows. You have collected all my tears in your bottle. You have recorded each one in your book."* He knows every betrayal, every broken trust, and every moment of hurt you have experienced. And God is not asking you to walk this road of healing alone. He is with you, ready to bind up your wounds and carry your burdens.

Letting go is also about breaking the fear that keeps you guarded. Toxic relationships and betrayals can leave you afraid to trust again, afraid to be vulnerable. But ladies, remember, fear is not your portion. As you let go of the past, God will give you the courage to open your heart to the right relationships and the wisdom to guard it against the wrong ones.

Forgiveness is a process, not a one-time event. It starts with a decision to forgive and continues as you bring the pain to God daily, asking Him to replace it with His peace. Practical steps like writing down what you are letting go of or praying for the person who hurt you can help solidify the act of release. Remember, this is not about excusing the offense. It is about refusing to let it control you any longer.

Let me share a little about my forgiveness journey with you. I came to understand that forgiveness has multiple layers. First, I had to ask God to forgive me. Then, I had to take the courageous step of forgiving myself. But the greatest test came when I had to forgive others, especially those who never apologized, kept lying, or showed no remorse. It was then that I truly grasped this powerful truth: forgiveness is for me, not for them. While I was waiting for them to acknowledge their wrongs, they had already moved on. I was the one still carrying the weight.

In my own way, I developed a process to forgive others, or so I thought. I would run to God and plead for help to forgive quickly, knowing that the longer I sat with the pain, the harder it would be to let go. And while I believed I had forgiven, I could not deny that twist in my gut, the way my spirit turned inside out whenever I saw the person or even heard their name. I might have smiled on the outside, but only God and I knew what I was really feeling on the inside.

Because I knew God cared more about the condition of my heart than my performance, I sought Him for years, asking why my heart and mind seemed out of sync when it came to forgiveness. And then, one day, it hit me—I had never asked God to heal my heart. I had forgiven, but I had not received healing. That was the missing piece.

So, I encourage you to not stop at forgiveness. Go further. Invite God to heal the parts of your heart that still ache. Forgiveness may release the burden, but healing restores the soul.

Finally, envision the freedom God has for you. Imagine waking up without the weight of bitterness, walking into new relationships without the fear of betrayal, and serving others with a heart full of love instead of guardedness. The peace of God is available to you when you trust God with the hurts you have been holding onto.

Letting go definitely does not mean forgetting. It means trusting God to bring justice, healing, and restoration. And as you release the past, you will find yourself stepping into the life of freedom, joy, and purpose God has been waiting to give you.

Acknowledging the Pain to Begin Healing

Let's start where all healing begins, with honesty. Before you can release the hurt or forgive, you must first acknowledge the pain. Ignoring it, suppressing it, or pretending it does not exist only gives it more power over your heart. God does not ask you to minimize your pain; He invites you to bring it to Him, raw and real, so He can begin the work of healing.

Too often, we try to push past the hurt with busyness or even spiritual platitudes. We tell ourselves, "It's fine," or "I have moved on," when deep down, the wound still aches. But healing requires bringing those broken places into the light. God meets you in your pain, not to rush you past it, but to walk with you through it.

Acknowledging the pain does not mean wallowing in it. It means naming it for what it is, a betrayal, a loss, a broken trust, and inviting God into that space. Jesus Himself demonstrated this. In John 11:35, we see the shortest verse in the Bible: *"Jesus wept."* He wept over the loss of His friend Lazarus, even though He knew resurrection was coming. His tears show us that acknowledging grief and pain is not a lack of faith; it is an act of faith that trusts God with the depths of our emotions.

Practical Step:

Take a moment to reflect on the pain you have been carrying. Write down every hurt, betrayal, or toxic relationship that has left a mark on your heart. Be honest with God about how it has affected you. Speak it out in prayer or even through journaling. Let Him know, *"Lord, this is where I'm hurting, and I need Your help to heal."*

_____

_____

_____

As you acknowledge the pain, resist the temptation to carry it alone. God invites you to lay your burdens at His feet, trusting that He is both willing and able to carry them for you.

Acknowledging the pain is not a sign of weakness. It is a step toward freedom. When you bring your hurt into the light of God's presence, you create space for Him to bind up your wounds and replace your bitterness with His peace. In that process, you will discover that God is not only close to the brokenhearted; He is the one who makes them whole.

Naming the Hurt to Take Its Power Away

Now, one of the most powerful steps in your healing journey is naming the hurt you have been carrying. It may seem simple, but giving your pain a name, identifying the betrayal, the loss, or the broken trust, takes away its power to silently control you. When you name the hurt, you bring it into the light where God can begin to heal it.

Unspoken pain has a way of lingering in the shadows, whispering lies about your worth, your future, and even God's goodness. But I am here to remind you that God sees every tear and knows every wound. When you name the hurt, you are not informing God of something He does not already know. You are inviting Him into that space to bring comfort and restoration.

Sometimes, we avoid naming the hurt because we think it makes us weak or unfaithful. But friend, even Jesus named His pain. On the cross, He cried out, *"My God, my God, why have you forsaken me?"* (Matthew 27:46). In that moment, Jesus acknowledged the depth of His suffering, showing us that bringing our pain to God is an act of trust, not a lack of faith.

Practical Step:

Find a quiet space where you will not be interrupted. Reflect on the hurt you have been carrying and write it down. Be specific. Name the relationship, the betrayal, or the situation that caused the pain. Then, speak it aloud in prayer: *"Lord, this is where I'm hurting. This is what happened, and this is how it's affected me. I need Your help to heal."*

_____

_____

_____

As you name the hurt, you may feel a wave of emotions, tears, anger, or even relief. Let it come. These emotions are part of releasing what you've been holding onto. Remember, friend, you are not alone at this moment. God is with you, ready to take the burden you have been carrying for far too long.

Naming the hurt does not mean you have all the answers or that the pain disappears instantly. But it does mean you have taken a bold step toward freedom. You have exposed the lie that says you must carry this alone, and you have opened the door for God to bring healing and peace into the broken places of your heart.

Releasing the Pain into God's Hands

Once you have named the hurt, the next step is releasing it into God's hands. Holding onto the pain might feel like a way to protect yourself, but in reality, it keeps you tied to the very thing that wounded you. Releasing the pain does not mean forgetting what happened or pretending it did not hurt. It means trusting God to carry what you no longer can.

Releasing your pain is an act of faith. It's saying, *"God, I trust You to heal my heart, to bring justice where it's needed, and to lead me into freedom."* The same God who holds the stars in place cares about every hurt you have experienced, and He is ready to take it from you if you will let Him.

Sometimes, we resist releasing pain because we feel like it gives power back to the person who hurt us. Releasing it is not about them. It is all about you. Romans 12:19 says, *"Do not take revenge, my dear friends, but leave room for God's wrath, for it is written: 'It is mine to avenge; I will repay,' says the Lord."* Letting go does not mean justice will not come; it means you are trusting God to handle it His way, in His time.

Practical Step:

Try a symbolic act of release. Write down the pain or offense on a piece of paper, and then physically release it, tear it up, burn it (safely), or place it in a box as a sign of surrendering it to God. As you do this, pray: *"Lord, I release this pain to You. I trust You to heal my heart and to bring justice in Your perfect way. Help me walk in the freedom You've promised."*

Releasing the pain does not mean you will never feel it again, but it does mean you are no longer holding onto it as your responsibility to resolve. It is a process, and some days you may need to release it again. But each time you do, you choose freedom over bitterness and faith over fear.

God is faithful, and when you release the pain to Him, He does not just carry it, He transforms it. He takes the broken pieces and creates something beautiful, something you could not imagine while you were still holding on. Trust God with your pain and watch as He turns it into something that brings healing and hope not only to you but also to others.

Embracing Forgiveness to Break Free

Now, the final step in letting go of past hurts is forgiveness. I know it's not easy. Forgiveness can feel like letting the person who hurt you off the hook, but that is not what it is. Forgiveness is not about excusing the offense; it's about refusing to let it control you any longer. It is a choice to release the bitterness and anger that weigh you down so you can live free.

Forgiveness is one of the most powerful gifts you can give yourself. Ephesians 4:31-32 reminds us, *"Get rid of all bitterness, rage and anger, brawling and slander, along with every form of malice. Be kind and compassionate to one another, forgiving each other, just as in Christ God*

73

forgave you." God calls us to forgive because He knows that holding onto resentment chains us to the past and blocks the peace, He wants us to have.

Choosing to forgive does not mean the pain instantly disappears. Forgiveness is a process, not a one-time event. It begins with a decision and continues as you bring the pain to God over and over, asking Him to soften your heart and replace the bitterness with His love. Matthew 6:14-15 says, "*For if you forgive other people when they sin against you, your heavenly Father will also forgive you. But if you do not forgive others their sins, your Father will not forgive your sins.*" Forgiveness is a reflection of God's grace in our lives, a grace that has no limits.

Practical Step:

Start by praying for the person who hurt you. Yes, it might feel impossible at first, but prayer is a powerful tool to shift your heart. Pray for their well-being, for God's work in their life, and for the ability to release the offense. If you are not ready to pray for them directly, begin by asking God to help you want to forgive. Write their name in your journal and release them into God's hands with a simple prayer: "*Lord, I choose to forgive. Help me to fully let go and trust You with the outcome.*"

Forgiveness does not mean forgetting or reopening doors that God has closed. It's about closing the chapter in your heart, so it no longer defines you. Philippians 3:13-14 encourages us, "*Forgetting what is behind and straining toward what is ahead, I press on toward the goal to win the prize for which God has called me heavenward in Christ Jesus.*"

Forgiveness elevates our freedom! It breaks the chains of resentment and opens the door for healing, peace, and even joy. As you embrace forgiveness, you will discover that it's not just about releasing someone else, but it is about releasing yourself. It's about stepping into the fullness of life that God has for you, unburdened by the weight of the past. And in that freedom, you will find the strength to love, to trust, and to live boldly once again.

Rebuilding Trust with Others and Yourself

Letting go of the past may hurt, and embracing forgiveness is a monumental step, but it often leaves a lingering question: How do I trust again? Trust, once broken, can feel impossible to rebuild, whether with others or even with yourself. But let me assure you, rebuilding trust is not just possible; it's part of the freedom and restoration God has for you.

Let's start with others. When someone has betrayed or hurt you, trusting again can feel like opening yourself up to be wounded all over again. But rebuilding trust does not mean throwing caution to the wind; it means walking in wisdom and discernment. Proverbs 3:5-6 reminds us, "Trust in the Lord with all your heart and lean not on your own understanding; in all your ways submit to him, and he will make your paths straight." Trusting God first allows Him to guide your steps as you navigate relationships.

Rebuilding trust with others begins with boundaries. Remember, boundaries are not barriers. They are tools to protect your heart while allowing space for healing and growth. Jesus Himself set boundaries in relationships. He loved all, but He did not entrust Himself to everyone. John 2:24 says, "But Jesus would not entrust himself to them, for he knew all people." Boundaries are a way to honor the work God is doing in your heart while ensuring that trust is earned over time, not blindly given.

Now, let's talk about trusting yourself. When you have been hurt, especially in toxic relationships, you may begin to doubt your own judgment, wondering how you allowed yourself to be in such a situation. Rebuilding trust with yourself starts with extending the same grace to yourself that God freely gives. Psalm 103:12 says, "As far as the east is from the west, so far has he removed our transgressions from us." If God does not hold your past against you, why should you?

Rebuilding self-trust also means learning to listen to the Holy Spirit within you. John 16:13 says, "But when he, the Spirit of truth, comes, he will guide you into all the truth." As you grow in your relationship with God, you will learn to discern His voice and trust the wisdom He imparts to you.

Practical Step:

Start small. In relationships, allow trust to rebuild gradually through consistent actions, honest communication, and prayer. For yourself, begin by reflecting on decisions you have made that align with God's will, and celebrate those moments as evidence of your growing discernment.

Rebuilding trust takes time, but it's worth the effort. Trusting others and yourself does not mean you will not encounter challenges again; it means you are walking forward with wisdom, courage, and the confidence that God is with you every step of the way. Guard your heart, not by closing it off, but by entrusting it fully to God as He restores your ability to trust again.

Rebuilding Trust with Others through Wisdom and Discernment

Trusting others again after being hurt is not easy. It's natural to feel guarded or hesitant, especially if you have been betrayed. But rebuilding trust does not mean opening yourself up to everyone without boundaries; it means walking forward with wisdom and discernment, allowing God to guide your steps.

The Bible reminds us in Proverbs 3:5-6, *"Trust in the Lord with all your heart and lean not on your own understanding; in all your ways submit to him, and he will make your paths straight."* Trusting God first allows Him to lead you in rebuilding relationships, whether with someone who has hurt you or in forming new connections.

Rebuilding trust with others begins with setting healthy boundaries. Boundaries create a space where healing can happen without leaving your heart vulnerable to further harm. Jesus set an example of boundaries in His relationships—He loved everyone, but He did not entrust Himself to everyone. You, too, can love others while being wise about who you allow into your inner circle.

Practical Step:

Start by observing actions over words. Trust is not rebuilt overnight; it grows through consistent, trustworthy behavior. Pray for discernment, asking God to reveal whether someone is truly committed to restoring the relationship. Remember, forgiveness is given freely, but trust is earned over time.

Rebuilding trust with others is not about rushing the process; it's about allowing God to lead you step by step. As you rely on His wisdom, you will find the courage to trust again, not out of fear, but with the confidence that He is protecting your heart.

Restoring Trust in Yourself by Embracing Grace

It's easy to question your own judgment. You might find yourself thinking, *"How did I not see this coming?"* or *"Can I trust myself to make better decisions in the future?"* But can I remind you of something? God's grace covers every mistake, and His Spirit empowers you to grow in wisdom and discernment. After all, if God does not hold your past against you, why should you? Rebuilding self-trust begins with extending the same grace to yourself that God has already given.

Practical Step:

Reflect on past decisions where you followed God's leading and saw good fruit. Celebrate those moments as reminders that you can trust yourself when you are walking in step with Him. Write them down and revisit them whenever self-doubt creeps in.

Trusting yourself again is not about being perfect; it's about learning, growing, and walking in alignment with God. With each step, you will discover that His grace is sufficient, and His Spirit is equipping you to walk boldly and confidently into your future.

Walking in Freedom by Trusting God Above All

Finally, rebuilding trust, whether with others or yourself, ultimately comes down to trusting God above all. People may fail you, and you may fail yourself, but God never will. Trusting Him is the foundation for every other relationship, including the one you have with yourself.

Proverbs 18:10 says, "The name of the Lord is a fortified tower; the righteous run to it and are safe." When you place your trust in God, you have an unshakable refuge. Even when relationships falter, or you doubt your own abilities, He remains your constant source of strength and wisdom.

Practical Step:

Make trusting God a daily habit. Start your day with a prayer of surrender: *"Lord, I trust You with my relationships, my decisions, and my heart. Guide me, protect me, and help me walk in Your wisdom."* As you consistently place your trust in Him, you will find that your confidence in others and you will begin to grow naturally.

Again, trusting God does not mean you will not face challenges, but it does mean you can navigate them with peace, knowing that He is in control. Isaiah 26:3 promises, *"You will keep in perfect peace those whose minds are steadfast, because they trust in you."* Friend, that peace is available to you as you lean on Him in every area of your life.

When you anchor your trust in God, you will find that rebuilding trust with others and yourself becomes less daunting. He will guide you, strengthen you, and lead you into the freedom and confidence that comes from knowing your life is held securely in His hands.

Chains to Freedom

If you have made it this far, you have already taken powerful step toward breaking the chains that have tried to hold you back far too long. Letting go of past hurts, toxic relationships, and bitterness is not an easy journey; it's a brave one. And the freedom you are stepping into is absolutely worth every ounce of surrender.

You were never created to live shackled to betrayal, disappointment, or fear. Jesus paid too high a price for you to live bound by anything less than the full, abundant life He promised. John 10:10 reminds us, *"I have come that they may have life, and have it to the full."* That full life starts the moment you choose to release the offenses of the past and embrace the healing and restoration God freely offers.

Forgiveness is not about forgetting or pretending it didn't hurt; it's about refusing to allow the pain to define you any longer. It is a decision to trust God with your wounds and believe that He will bring beauty from your ashes. Isaiah 61:3 isn't just a nice verse; it's your reality when you lay your pain at His feet: *"To give them a crown of beauty for ashes, the oil of joy instead of mourning, and a garment of praise instead of a spirit of despair."*

As you rebuild trust with others and with yourself, know that God is your foundation. People may fail you. Even your own heart may doubt. But God never fails. Proverbs 3:5-6 is your anchor: *"Trust in the Lord with all your heart and lean not on your own understanding; in all your ways submit to him, and he will make your paths straight."*

Practical Step:

Own these declarations over your life today:
- *I choose to release the pain of the past.*
- *I choose to forgive, not because they deserve it, but because I deserve peace.*
- *I choose to trust again, with God leading and guarding my heart.*

You are not stepping forward alone; God is walking every step with you. He is healing places you thought were too broken and strengthening your heart for the beautiful future ahead.

So, rise up and walk in your purpose and your power!

Leave behind the weight that was never yours to carry.

Step boldly into the freedom, peace, and overflowing joy that God has already prepared for you.

Because when you release the chains of the past, you don't just walk; you soar!

CHAPTER SEVEN

Rising Strong: Embracing Your Purpose and Walking in Power

Living Authentically, Boldly, and Impactfully for God's Glory

As we come to the final chapter of this journey, I want you to take a moment to pause and reflect on how far you have come. You have faced your past, released the weight of pain and bitterness, rebuilt trust, and silenced the lies that tried to hold you back. Now, it is time to rise, to step boldly into the purpose and power God has placed within you.

Living fully in your God-given identity is not just about knowing who you are. It's about embracing it with courage and clarity. You are not who your past says you are; you are who God says you are. Friend, you have been called out of darkness, and now it is time to shine.

Embracing your purpose requires alignment - aligning your gifts, passions, and priorities with God's plan for your life. It is about living intentionally, not just for yourself, but for the impact you are meant to have on others. Ephesians 2:10 tells us, *"For we are God's handiwork, created in Christ Jesus to do good works, which God prepared in advance for us to do."* There are people, opportunities, and missions waiting for you to step boldly into.

Walking in power does not mean you will never feel fear. It means you will choose faith over fear. Joshua 1:9 encourages us, *"Have I not commanded you? Be strong and courageous. Do not be afraid; do not be discouraged, for the Lord your God will be with you wherever you go."* God's presence goes with you as you take each step forward. You do not have to have everything figured out; you just have to trust Him to lead you.

This chapter is about turning transformation into action. It's about taking the lessons you have learned and the healing you have experienced and using them as fuel to live boldly. Whether in your family, your work, your community, or your ministry, you are called to lead, inspire, and uplift. Your journey is not just for you. It is a testimony of God's power and a light for others who are still searching for hope.

Practical Step:

Start by creating a vision for your future. Ask God to reveal His plan for the next chapter of your life. Write it down, pray over it, and take one small step each day toward that vision.

Step One

_____

_____

_____

Surround yourself with a community that uplifts and supports you and never stop seeking God's guidance in everything you do.

Rising strong means choosing to live fully and boldly in the freedom and purpose God has given you. It means leading with authenticity, loving with grace, and serving with joy. This is your time to shine, not because of who you are but because of who He is in you. You are not just stepping into a new chapter. You are stepping into a new life filled with purpose, power, and impact.

So, rise, my friend! The world is waiting for the light that only you can bring.

Overcoming the Fear of Rejection by Trusting God's Acceptance

One of the greatest fears that holds us back from living authentically is the fear of rejection. What if they do not accept the real me? What if I am not enough? These questions often keep us hiding behind masks, afraid to show the world who we truly are. But can I remind you of something powerful? Your worth is not determined by others' opinions. It is defined by God's love.

Ephesians 1:4-5 reminds us, *"For he chose us in him before the creation of the world to be holy and blameless in his sight. In love he predestined us for adoption to sonship through Jesus Christ, in accordance with his pleasure and will."* Before the world even knew you, God chose you. He loved you fully and unconditionally. And because His acceptance is eternal, you do not have to live for the fleeting approval of others.

The fear of rejection often whispers that being vulnerable will lead to hurt. But living authentically means trusting that God's acceptance is greater than any rejection you may face. John 15:18 reminds us, *"If the world hates you, keep in mind that it hated me first."* Jesus Himself faced rejection, yet He stayed true to His mission, knowing His worth was rooted in the Father's love.

Practical Step:

When you feel the fear of rejection creeping in, pause and declare a truth over yourself: *"I am loved, chosen, and accepted by God."* Write down Ephesians 1:4-5 and keep it where you can see it daily, as a reminder that His love and approval are more than enough.

Overcoming the fear of rejection does not mean everyone will embrace you. But it does mean you will live free from the chains of people-pleasing and self-doubt. As you rest in God's acceptance, you will find the courage to be your authentic self, knowing that the One who matters most already calls you His own.

Releasing the Fear of Judgment by Resting in God's Truth

Another roadblock to living authentically is the fear of judgment. You might think, *"What will people say if I let them see the real me?"* or *"What if they misunderstand or criticize me?"* But here is the truth: living authentically means prioritizing God's opinion over people's opinions. And let me tell you, God's truth about you is far greater than any judgment this world could ever offer.

Romans 8:31 reminds us, *"If God is for us, who can be against us?"* When you live authentically, rooted in His purpose and design, no criticism can diminish your value or worth. People may have opinions, but they do not have the power to define you. Only God does.

The fear of judgment often keeps us striving for perfection, thinking that if we are flawless, no one will have anything negative to say. But perfection is not God's standard. Faithfulness is. When you embrace your flaws and lean on His grace, you reflect His strength and authenticity, not your own striving.

Practical Step:

Start practicing the habit of releasing judgment to God. When you feel the fear of being misunderstood or criticized, pray: *"Lord, I surrender the opinions of others to You. Help me to rest in the truth of who You say I am."* Write down a list of truths from Scripture about your identity in Christ and declare them over yourself whenever fear arises.

_____

_____

_____

Releasing the fear of judgment is a daily choice, but it is one that brings freedom and peace. When you focus on God's truth, you will find that the opinions of others lose their power over you. And as you rest in His love and approval, you will walk boldly in your authenticity, knowing that your life is a reflection of His glory, not anyone else's expectations.

Embracing Vulnerability as a Strength, Not a Weakness

Living authentically means being willing to show your heart and be vulnerable, even when it feels risky. The world often tells us that vulnerability is a sign of weakness, but God sees vulnerability as a strength. When you are open about your struggles, your fears, and even your imperfections, you allow His power to shine through you.

Vulnerability is not about exposing yourself for no reason; it is about creating space for God's strength to be made visible in your life. Embracing vulnerability also invites a deeper connection with others. The moments when you let your guard down are often the moments when people feel most inspired and connected to you. Sharing your authentic self creates an opportunity for mutual encouragement and growth.

Practical Step:

Start small. Share one area of your life where you have been hesitant to be vulnerable, whether it's a fear, a dream, or a struggle, with someone you trust. Pray beforehand, asking God to guide your words and to use your vulnerability as a source of strength for both you and the person you share with.

Vulnerability is not about being weak. It is about being real. When you choose to live authentically, imperfections and all, you reflect the beauty of God's grace working through you. And as you embrace vulnerability, you will discover a newfound strength and freedom that comes from living in the fullness of who He created you to be.

Courageously Stepping Into Your Purpose

Now that you have embraced your authentic self, the next step is stepping boldly into the purpose God has uniquely designed for you. Your purpose is not just about what you do. It's about who you are in Christ and how you live out His calling in every aspect of your life. Stepping into this purpose requires courage, clarity, and a willingness to trust God with every step forward.

Stepping into your purpose begins with believing that you were created for a reason. You were intentionally designed by God to make an impact, not by striving but by aligning your gifts, passions, and opportunities with His plan.

But let's be honest: stepping into your purpose can feel intimidating. Fear of failure, self-doubt, or not knowing where to start can keep you from moving forward. That is why courage is key.

Clarity is another essential part of living out your purpose. Purpose does not happen by accident; it is cultivated through prayer, reflection, and intentional action. Proverbs 16:3 says, *"Commit to the Lord whatever you do, and he will establish your plans."* As you align your priorities and decisions with His will, He will direct your path and open doors you could not imagine!

Practical Step:

Take time to reflect on the gifts, talents, and passions God has placed in your heart. Write them down and ask Him to reveal how they align with His purpose for your life.

_____

_____

_____

Pray over your list and take one small step toward living out your purpose, whether it is saying "yes" to an opportunity, reaching out to someone for guidance, or dedicating time to a project you've been called to start.

Stepping into your purpose is not about perfection but about faithfulness. As you walk boldly in your calling, you will discover that

God's strength is made perfect in your weakness, and His grace is sufficient for every challenge you face. Your journey will inspire others, not because you are perfect, but because you are faithful.

Remember, your purpose is bigger than you. It's about impacting the world around you with the love, grace, and truth of God. Philippians 2:13 reminds us, *"For it is God who works in you to will and to act in order to fulfill his good purpose."* Trust Him to lead you and watch as He uses your life to bring hope, healing, and transformation to others.

Discovering Your God-Given Gifts and Passions

Stepping into your purpose begins with understanding the unique gifts and passions God has placed within you. These are not random talents or interests; they are intentional tools designed to help you fulfill the good works He prepared for you. Your gifts and passions are part of that handiwork, carefully crafted to bring glory to Him and impact others.

Sometimes, we overlook our gifts because they feel ordinary to us, but friend, what feels natural to you may be extraordinary to someone else. Romans 12:6 says, *"We have different gifts, according to the grace given to each of us."* Whether your gift is teaching, serving, encouraging, leading, creating, or something else entirely, it is valuable in the Kingdom of God.

Discovering your gifts and passions starts with reflection. Ask yourself:

1. *What activities or tasks bring me joy and fulfillment?*
2. *What comes naturally to me, and where do others often seek my help or advice?*
3. *Where have I seen God use me to make a difference in the past?*

_____

_____

_____

Practical Step:

Friend, God does not give gifts without a purpose. 1 Peter 4:10 says, *"Each of you should use whatever gift you have received to serve others, as faithful stewards of God's grace in its various forms."* As you discover and embrace your unique design, you will begin to see how your gifts and passions fit into the bigger picture of His plan.

Your gifts are not just for you; they are a way for God to work through you to bless others. Do not hide them or underestimate them. Instead, trust that the God who created you will use every part of you to bring hope, healing, and transformation to those around you.

Aligning Your Gifts with God's Purpose

Discovering your gifts is only the beginning. The next step is aligning those gifts with God's purpose for your life. Alignment is about taking the talents, passions, and abilities God has placed within you and using them to serve and glorify Him. It is about saying "yes" to His plan, even when it feels bigger than you or stretches you in ways you did not expect.

God's purpose for your life is not random or unclear; He has a plan, and He wants you to walk in it. When you align your gifts with His purpose, you step into the joy, fulfillment, and peace that come from living in His will.

Alignment requires surrender. It means letting go of your own plans and asking God to direct your path. Proverbs 3:5-6 encourages us, *"Trust in the Lord with all your heart and lean not on your own understanding; in all your ways submit to him, and he will make your paths straight."* Trusting God's purpose may feel risky, but His plans are always better than anything we could imagine.

Practical Step:

Take time to pray and reflect on how your gifts can be used to serve others and advance God's Kingdom. Write down specific ways you can use your talents in your family, community, church, or workplace. Look for opportunities that align with your passions and strengths and take one actionable step this week to walk in alignment with God's plan.

Aligning your gifts with God's purpose is not about striving but obedience. It's about saying, *"Lord, use me however You will,"* and trusting Him to open the right doors at the right time. Ephesians 3:20 reminds us, *"Now to him who is able to do immeasurably more than all we ask or imagine, according to his power that is at work within us."* When you align your gifts with His purpose, you will discover that His power working through you is greater than any limitation or fear.

Living in alignment is a journey, not a destination. As you continue to seek Him, He will guide you, refine you, and use you in ways that exceed your expectations. Trust Him with your gifts and watch as He transforms your obedience into impact.

Taking Bold Action to Walk in Your Calling

After discovering your gifts and aligning them with God's purpose, the final step is taking bold action. Purpose is not just about knowing. It is about doing. It is about stepping out in faith, trusting that God will equip you as you go. James 2:17 reminds us, *"Faith by itself, if it is not accompanied by action, is dead."* Your gifts and purpose come alive when you move from reflection to action.

Taking bold action does not mean you won't feel fear. It means you will trust God more than your fear. Joshua 1:9 encourages us, *"Have I not commanded you? Be strong and courageous. Do not be afraid; do not be discouraged, for the Lord your God will be with you wherever you go."* Friend, you are not alone on this journey. God is with you, guiding your steps and strengthening you as you walk forward.

Sometimes, the hardest part of taking action is the first step. You might wonder, *"What if I fail?"* or *"What if I'm not ready?"* But can I remind you? God does not call the equipped; He equips the called. 2 Corinthians 3:5 says, *"Not that we are competent in ourselves to claim anything for ourselves, but our competence comes from God."* Your job is not to have it all figured out; it is to take the next step in obedience and trust God with the results.

Practical Step:

Write down one actionable goal that aligns with your purpose, something that feels just outside your comfort zone but excites you. Pray over it and commit to taking that step this week, whether it is starting a project, reaching out to someone for guidance, or sharing your story with others.

_____

_____

_____

Bold action does not mean rushing ahead without direction. It means listening to God's voice and following where He leads. Isaiah 30:21 promises, *"Whether you turn to the right or to the left, your ears will hear a voice behind you, saying, 'This is the way; walk in it."* Trust that God will guide you, even if the path feels uncertain.

As you take action, remember that success is not measured by the outcome but by your obedience. Every step of faith is an act of worship, a declaration that you trust God's plan more than your own doubts. And as you walk in your calling, you will discover a strength, joy, and fulfillment that only comes from living in alignment with His purpose.

This is your moment to rise. Take the step, trust the process, and watch as God works through you in ways you never imagined.

Rising Strong in Purpose and Power

Friend, as we close this chapter and this incredible journey together, I want you to take a moment to reflect on all that God has done in your heart. You have faced your past, released the pain that once held you back, rebuilt trust, silenced the inner critic, and embraced your authentic self. And now, you are ready to rise, to step boldly into the purpose and power God has uniquely designed for you.

Rising strong is not about perfection; it is about faith. It's about trusting that the same God who carried you through the storms will also equip you to live fully in your calling. The work God has started in you is only the beginning. He has so much more ahead.

Stepping into your purpose means living authentically, embracing the gifts God has placed within you, and taking bold action to walk in your calling. It means showing up as the woman God created you to be, unapologetically and with courage. Friend, your story matters. Your gifts matter. Your purpose matters. And God has equipped you for every step of the journey.

Remember, you do not have to have all the answers or see the entire path ahead. Trust Him to guide you, and He will lead you into places that exceed your expectations.

Practical Step:

Write a declaration of commitment to living boldly in your purpose. Start with,

"I am choosing to rise..." and finish with what you are stepping into, your calling, your gifts, and your trust in God. Speak it over yourself daily as a reminder of the life you are walking into.

I am Choosing to Rise:

Today, I release _____.
I forgive _____.
I choose to walk in _____.
I believe that God is _____

.
And today, I step into _____.

Friend, your words carry life. Speak them boldly.

Revisit this declaration as often as needed, especially when old storms try to rise again.

As you rise, know that your journey does not end here. This is only the beginning. God has called you, equipped you, and prepared you to make an impact in the world. Walk in His strength, lean into His guidance, and never forget that He is with you every step of the way.

This is your time to rise. The world is waiting for the light, love, and transformation that only you can bring. Go boldly, friend, and live the life God has called you to, one filled with purpose, power, and a legacy of faith!

Prayer Declaration: Walking Boldly in Freedom

Father God, I come before You today with an open heart, fully surrendering every hurt, every fear, and every burden I have carried. Thank You for being the God who sees, who knows, and who heals. I declare that I am no longer bound by the chains of past pain, guilt, or comparison.

Today, I choose freedom.

Today, I choose to trust You more than my fears.

Today, I release the need to strive for perfection and instead walk boldly in the grace You have already given me.

Lord, teach me to serve from overflow, not exhaustion.

Strengthen me to set boundaries that honor the calling You have placed on my life.

Silence every lie of the enemy with the truth of Your Word planted deep in my spirit.

I declare that I am fearfully and wonderfully made.

I am called.

I am equipped.

I am unstoppable because You are my strength and my guide.

I trust You with my relationships, my decisions, my dreams, and my future.

Where fear once lived, faith now rises.

Where pain once paralyzed, Your purpose now propels me forward.

I embrace my true identity in Christ. I will walk boldly into my destiny with joy, with courage, and with unstoppable faith.

In Jesus' Name,

Amen.

Remember, YOU are no longer a whisper of past storms.
You are the living, breathing evidence of God's unstoppable purpose and power, and I am so proud of YOU!

Your Friend,
Yvonne Lorraine

Scripture Index

Organized for Reflection, Application, and Prayer

This index is your go-to for finding the Scriptures that shaped each chapter of this book. Use it to revisit key promises, meditate on God's truth, and go deeper in your own personal study and healing journey.

Chapter One

- *Romans 8:1 – There is now no condemnation for those in Christ Jesus. (Freedom from Shame)*
- *2 Corinthians 5:17 – If anyone is in Christ, the new creation has come. (New Identity)*
- *Isaiah 43:18-19 – Forget the former things. I am doing a new thing. (Fresh Start)*
- *Philippians 1:6 – He who began a good work in you will carry it on. (Ongoing Transformation)*
- *Romans 12:2 – Be transformed by the renewing of your mind. (Mindset Shift)*
- *Psalm 34:5 – Those who look to Him are radiant. (Unashamed Confidence)*
- *Galatians 2:20 – I no longer live, but Christ lives in me. (Christ-Centered Life)*
- *Jeremiah 29:11 – Plans to prosper you, not to harm you. (Hope for the Future)*

Chapter Two

- *Romans 8:28 – All things work together for good. (Divine Purpose in Pain)*
- *John 16:33 – In this world, you will have trouble... But take heart! (Peace in the Storm)*
- *2 Corinthians 4:17 – Light and momentary troubles. (Eternal Glory Perspective)*
- *Psalm 147:3 – He heals the brokenhearted. (Emotional Healing)*
- *Isaiah 41:10 – Do not fear, for I am with you. (God's Presence)*

- *Romans 5:3-5 – Suffering produces perseverance... (Growth through Trials)*
- *Lamentations 3:22-23 – His mercies are new every morning. (Daily Grace)*

Chapter Three

- *Proverbs 3:5-6 – Trust in the Lord with all your heart. (Divine Direction)*
- *Psalm 23:1-3 – He leads me beside quiet waters. (Restoration)*
- *Matthew 11:28-30 – Come to Me and I will give you rest. (Soul Rest)*
- *Exodus 14:14 – The Lord will fight for you. (Letting Go of Control)*
- *Philippians 4:6-7 – Do not be anxious... (Peace through Prayer)*
- *Mark 1:35 – Jesus withdrew to pray. (Rhythm of Rest)*
- *Hebrews 4:9-11 – There remains a Sabbath-rest. (Sacred Rest)*

Chapter Four

- *Proverbs 4:23 – Guard your heart. (Emotional Protection)*
- *Galatians 5:22-23 – Fruit of the Spirit. (Emotional Evidence)*
- *Psalm 139:23-24 – Search me, God. (Emotional Honesty)*
- *Ephesians 4:26 – In your anger, do not sin. (Righteous Boundaries)*
- *2 Corinthians 10:5 – Take captive every thought. (Mental Mastery)*
- *James 1:5 – Ask God for wisdom. (Clarity in Conflict)*
- *John 8:32 – The truth will set you free. (Emotional Freedom)*

Chapter Five

- *Romans 12:1 – True Worship Through Aligned Sacrifice*
- *Romans 8:1 – Freedom from Condemnation*
- *Luke 5:16 – Withdrawing for Renewal*
- *Psalm 139:14 – Created with Worth and Intention*
- *Philippians 4:13 – Strength in Christ*
- *Proverbs 4:23 – Guarding the Heart*
- *John 15:5 – Fruitfulness Through Connection*
- *Exodus 20:8-10 – Honoring Rest*

- *Hebrews 12:1 – Staying in Your Lane*
- *Romans 12:6-8 – Operating in Your Gifts*
- *Isaiah 61:1 – Healing for the Brokenhearted*
- *John 10:10 – Abundant Life Over the Enemy's Lies*
- *2 Corinthians 12:9 – Grace in Weakness*
- *Ephesians 6:17 – Word as Your Weapon*
- *Psalm 46:1 – God is Your Refuge*

Chapter Six

- *Psalm 56:8 – God Sees Every Tear*
- *John 11:35 – Jesus Wept – Validating Grief*
- *Matthew 27:46 – Naming the Pain to Invite Healing*
- *Romans 12:19 – Letting God Handle Justice*
- *Matthew 6:14-15 – Forgiveness Reflects God's Grace*
- *Ephesians 4:31-32 – Freedom Through Forgiveness*
- *Philippians 3:13-14 – Moving Forward with Purpose*
- *Proverbs 3:5-6 – Trusting God to Rebuild Trust*
- *John 2:24 – Jesus Modeled Boundaries*
- *Psalm 103:12 – Grace Removes Guilt*
- *John 16:13 – Guidance by the Spirit*
- *Proverbs 18:10 – God is a Safe Refuge*
- *Isaiah 26:3 – Peace Through Trust*
- *John 10:10 – Abundant Life is Yours*
- *Isaiah 61:3 – Beauty for Ashes*

Chapter Seven

- *Ephesians 2:10 – Created for Purpose*
- *Joshua 1:9 – Courage to Move Forward*
- *Ephesians 1:4-5 – Chosen and Loved*
- *John 15:18 – Rejection is Not the End*

- *Romans 8:31 – God is for You*
- *Proverbs 16:3 – Commit, and He Will Establish*
- *Romans 12:6 – Grace-Filled Gifts*
- *1 Peter 4:10 – Stewarding Your Gift Well*
- *Proverbs 3:5-6 – Trusting God's Plan*
- *Ephesians 3:20 – God Can Do More Than You Imagine*
- *James 2:17 – Faith Requires Action*
- *2 Corinthians 3:5 – God is Your Competence*
- *Isaiah 30:21 – God Will Guide You*
- *Philippians 2:13 – God Works Through You*
- *Isaiah 61:3 – Beauty for Ashes*